Augsburg's Drawing

BOOK I.

A Text Book Designed to Teach Drawing and Color in the First, Second and Third Grades

BY

D. R. Augsburg

Director of Drawing in the Public Schools of Oakland, Cal.

Copyright © 2013 Read Books Ltd.
This book is copyright and may not be
reproduced or copied in any way without
the express permission of the publisher in writing

British Library Cataloguing-in-Publication Data
A catalogue record for this book is available from the
British Library

Drawing and Illustration

Drawing is a form of visual art that can make use of any number of drawing instruments, including graphite pencils, pen and ink, inked brushes, wax colour pencils, crayons, charcoal, chalk, pastels and various kinds of erasers, markers, styluses, metals (such as silverpoint) and even electronic drawing. As a medium, it has been one of the most popular and fundamental means of public expression throughout human history – as one of the simplest and most efficient means of communicating visual ideas.

Drawing itself long predates other forms of human communication, with evidence for its existence preceding that of the written word – demonstrated in cave paintings of around 40,000 years ago. These drawings, known as pictograms, depicted objects and abstract concepts including animals, human hands and generalised patterns. Over time, these sketches and paintings were stylised and simplified, leading to the development of the written language as we know it today. This form of drawing can truly be considered art in its purest sense – the basic forms on which all others build.

Whilst the term 'to draw' derives from the Old English *dragan* (meaning 'to drag, draw or protract'), the word 'illustrate' derives from the Latin word *illustratio,* meaning 'enlighten' or 'irradiate'. This process of 'enlightenment' is central to drawing and illustration as we know it today. Medieval codices' illustrations were often called 'illuminations', designed to highlight and further explain important aspects of biblical texts. This was the most general form of illustration; hand-created, individual and unique. This changed in the fifteenth century however, when books began to be illustrated with woodcuts – most notably in Germany, by Albrecht Dürer.

The first creative impulses of a painter or sculptor are commonly expressed in drawings, and architects and photographers are commonly trained to draw, if for no other reason than to train their perceptual skills and develop their creative potential. Initially, artists used and re-used wooden tablets for the production of their drawings, however following the widespread availability of paper in the fourteenth century, the use of drawing in the arts increased. During the Renaissance (a period of massive flourishing of human intellectual endeavours and creativity), drawings exhibiting realistic and representational qualities emerged. Notable draftsmen included Leonardo da Vinci, Michelangelo and Raphael. They were inspired by the concurrent developments in geometry and philosophy, exhibiting a true synthesis of these branches – a combination somewhat lost in the modern day.

Figure drawing became a recognised subsection of artistic drawing in this period, despite its long history stretching back to prehistoric descriptions. An anecdote by the Roman author and philosopher Pliny, describes how Zeuxis (a painter who flourished during the 5th century BCE) reviewed the young women of Agrigentum naked before selecting five whose features he would combine in order to paint an ideal image. The use of nude models in the medieval artist's workshop is further implied in the writings of Cennino Cennini (an Italian painter), and a manuscript of Villard de Honnecourt confirms that sketching from life was an established practice by the thirteenth century. The Carracci, who opened their *Accademia degli Incamminati* (one of the first art academies in Italy) in Bologna in the 1580s, set the pattern for later art schools by making life drawing the central discipline. The course of training began with the copying of engravings, then proceeded to drawing from plaster casts, after which the students were trained in drawing from the live model.

The main processes for reproduction of drawings and illustrations in the sixteenth and seventeenth centuries were engraving and etching, and by the end of the eighteenth century, lithography (a method of printing originally based on the immiscibility of oil and water) allowed even better illustrations to be reproduced. In the later seventeenth and eighteenth centuries, the previous combination of the arts and sciences in drawing gave way to a more romantic and even classical style, epitomised by draftsmen such as Poussin, Rembrandt, Rubens, Tiepolo and Antoine Watteau. Mastery in drawing was considered a prerequisite to painting, and students in Jacques-Louis David's Studio (a famed eighteenth century French painter of the neo-classical style), were required to draw for six hours a day, from a model who remained in the same pose for an entire week!

During this period, an increasingly large gap started to emerge between 'fine artists' on the one hand, and 'draftsmen' / 'illustrators' on the other. This difference became further complicated with the 'Golden Age of Illustration'; a period customarily defined as lasting from the latter quarter of the nineteenth century until just after the First World War. In this period of no more than fifty years the popularity, abundance and most importantly the unprecedented upsurge in quality of illustrated works marked an astounding change in the way that publishers, artists and the general public came to view artistic drawing. Arthur Rackham, Walter Crane, John Tenniel and William Blake are some of its most famous names. Until the latter part of the nineteenth century, the work of illustrators was largely proffered anonymously, and in England it was only after Thomas Bewick's pioneering technical advances in wood engraving that it became common to acknowledge the artistic and technical expertise of illustrators. Such draftsmen also frequently used their drawings in preparation for paintings, further obfuscating the distinction between drawing/painting, high/low art.

The artists involved in the Arts and Crafts Movement (with a strong emphasis on stylised drawing, and a powerful influence on the 'Golden Age of Illustration') also attempted to counter the ever intruding Industrial Revolution, by bringing the values of beautiful and inventive craftsmanship back into the sphere of everyday life. This helped to counter the main challenge which emerged around this time – photography. The invention of the first widely available form of photography (with flexible photographic film role marketed in 1885) led to a shift in the use of drawing in the arts. This new technology took over from drawing as a superior method of accurately representing the visual world, and many artists abandoned their painstaking drawing practices. As a result of these developments however, modernism in the arts emerged – encouraging 'imaginative originality' in drawing and abstract formulations. Drawing was once again at the forefront of the arts.

There are many different categories of drawing, including figure drawing, cartooning, doodling and shading. There are also many drawing methods, such as line drawing, stippling, shading, hatching, crosshatching, creating textures and tracing – and the artist must be aware of complex problems such as form, proportion and perspective (portrayed in either linear methods, or depth through tone and texture). Today, there are also many computer-aided drawing tools, which are utilised in design, architecture, engineering, as well as the fine arts. It is often exploratory, with considerable emphasis on observation, problem-solving and composition, and as such, remains an unceasingly useful tool in the artists repertoire.

The processes of drawing is a fascinating artistic practice, enabling a beautiful array of effects and creative expression. As is evident from this short introduction, it also has an incredibly old history, moving from decorations on cave walls to the most advanced, realistic and imaginative drawings possible in the present day. It is hoped that the current reader enjoys this book on the subject.

PREFACE.

"Augsburg's Drawing" is a Three Book System designed to teach Form and Color in the Public Schools. Each subject is treated topically, and arranged so as to give the widest latitude and the greatest flexibility in teaching.

Book I. is a Teachers' Hand Book showing simple and effective methods of teaching drawing, including color, to children in the first, second and third grades.

Book II. is designed as a regular text book to be placed in the hands of pupils of the fourth, fifth, sixth, seventh and eighth grades, and should be used the same as a text book in arithmetic or other subjects. It may also be used as a manual, in connection with a system of copy, blank books or drawing pads. Book II. forms a complete course of the essentials of Free-hand Drawing.

Book III. contains short, yet complete, courses in Brush Drawing, Wash Drawing, Water Color Drawing, Pen Drawing, Chalk Modeling, Drawing of the Human Head and Figure, Decorative Design and Mechanical Drawing. Book III. is to be used when any of the above subjects are taught. It is designed to enrich and make complete the subject of drawing.

CONTENTS.

	PAGE
GENERAL PRINCIPLES	7
FIRST YEARS OF DRAWING	13

CHAPTER I.
DRAWING FROM MEMORY AND THE IMAGINATION . . . 15

CHAPTER II.
ACTION DRAWING 21

CHAPTER III.
AMBIDEXTROUS OR TWO-HANDED DRAWING 35

CHAPTER IV.
PLACE AND RELATION OF OBJECTS 47

CHAPTER V.
THE DRAWING OF TREES 58

CHAPTER VI.
RELATIVE SIZE OF OBJECTS 70

CHAPTER VII.
TEACHING PROPORTION 76

CHAPTER VIII.
Teaching Unity 87

CHAPTER IX.
Primary Object Drawing 98

CHAPTER X.
Quick Drawing 115

CHAPTER XI.
The Drawing of Birds 125

CHAPTER XII.
The Drawing of Animals . . . . . , . 140

CHAPTER XIII.
Teaching Color 153

CHAPTER XIV.
Brush Drawing 160

CHAPTER XV.
Water Colors 170

INTRODUCTION.

GENERAL PRINCIPLES.

The Mental Image.—In drawing, the child does not draw directly from the object, but from the image of the object that is in his mind. It is the office of the model to stimulate, correct, and vivify this mental image. "This image is the great instrument of instruction," hence it should be one of the chief aims of the teacher to help the child form correct images; to train the child's power of imagery. Some of the principal sources of image-making are objects, both natural and artificial, pictures, poetry, oral pictures, stories, music, dramatic action, geography, history, science, etc. All of these may be used in the drawing-class. Especially should those sources of imagery be used that grow out of the life of the child, such as his games, plays, and sources of interest.

The Idea and Its Expression.—In every mode of expression there is (1) the idea, (2) the mode or method of expressing the idea. The mode of expressing the idea indicates the grasp the child has of it. The more complete the grasp of the idea the better will be the mode of expressing it. The idea and its expression should be as nearly a unit as possible. It is wrong to separate the mode of expression from the idea. A mode of expression without its idea — without something to express — is a waste of time, and will be barren of results. Expression is the following of a thought — the thought expressed. This thought, this idea or concept, is the real substance which expands into the visible drawing.

The Type Form.—The type form is a measure of comparison; a single object that is similar to or typical of many objects. The type form is useless to the child until he has something to measure with it — until he feels the need of it. The type form should be studied in connection with the objects of which it is a type. It should not supplant, but attend. The principal type forms in drawing are the sphere, cube, cylinder, and triangular prism. It is doubtful if type forms are of much use before the fourth grade.

Mediums of Expression.— There are many mediums of expression within the reach of the school-room. Some of them are the lead pencil, crayon, charcoal, water colors, clay modeling, paper cutting, brush drawing, pen drawing, knife work, etc. One is apt to look on these different means of expression as having little relation to each other, but this is not so, they may be different mediums for doing the same thing. The mechanical— the hand part of the work — differs in each, but the mental part is the same. That is, if one can draw (I do not mean copy) a kitten with a lead pencil, he can draw the kitten in crayon, charcoal, paint it in water colors, model it in clay, cut it from paper with scissors, draw it with a pen, or cut it from wood with a knife, *as soon as he has overcome the mechanical difficulties of working in each.* The idea remains unchanged in all modes of expression — it is eternal; the mechanical means is all that changes.

Lead Pencil and Water Color.— Perhaps the best and most practical mediums for use in the school-room are the lead pencil and water colors. Both of these are used universally, and in almost every department of life's work. The pencil is best suited to outline, and the water colors to the mass, and both may be used very effectively together.

Copying.— The copy, in teaching drawing, is useful chiefly in *showing how.* It is the "*how*" of drawing. It is not well to encourage pupils to copy drawings indiscriminately, or without a special object in view. It is a habit that is easily formed and will be very much abused if not guarded against. Rather use the copy to show the pupils *how*, and lead them to draw their own image, or ideas in the language of the copy. For example—the pupils are drawing acorns, at their seats. The teacher steps up to the blackboard and draws an acorn to show the pupils *how*, and to encourage them. They are not to copy her acorn, but to draw theirs in a similar manner. The copy is to show the method and reveal the principle. Without the copy we would not know the *mode of drawing*, for there is nothing in the object or idea to show how to represent it on a flat surface.

It is well to study all subjects in drawing under the three general heads of:

Imitation or Copy Drawing.
Perceptive or Object Drawing.
Imaginative and Memory Drawing.

Imitation or Copy Drawing is to impart the method, reveal the principle, to show how to use the medium and the various mechanical devices.

Perceptive or Object Drawing is to give ideas of form, color, relation, relative size, proportion, construction and to form and correct the mental image.

Imaginative and Memory Drawing is to give power to do, to express thought and impart ideas. To turn perceptive knowledge into conceptive knowledge and to make the mechanical processes largely automatic.

It will be seen from the above that in all drawing the object is *the source*, the copy is *the how*, and the memory is *the test*.

Generally these three classes of drawing should go hand in hand, each supporting, helping, and explaining the others.

Quick Drawing.— Drawing is not slow work. The only part that is slow is the *don't-know-how* part. Remove this, and the actual doing is quick and rapid. There is no place in the school-room for slow and laborious drawing. Each member of the class should begin and finish the drawing in one lesson, whether the lesson be ten or thirty minutes long. Time sketches are excellent to lead the pupil directly to the idea and forget the medium in which he is working.

Blackboard Drawing.—There is no medium equal to the blackboard for drill work. The largeness of the lines gives freedom, its publicity stimulates to effort and creates confidence. The teacher has a better opportunity to give directions and suggestions, and the change in medium gives variety. Blackboard drawing should be practiced systematically and regularly. There is no place on the blackboard for useless pictures and decorations. The blackboard is for daily use. Decorations and pictures may be placed there, but only for a purpose, and should be erased as soon as that purpose is accomplished.

Training the Hand.— The proper way to train the hand is through the mind. The hand is but the servant of the mind. It is the mental image that should be first. Aim to make this mental image vivid and strong and the hand will acquire its highest skill in producing it. Arm movements, counting movements, and all those exercises that throw the mind into a passive state, are not only wrong, but are an injurious waste of time. The mind is everything, the hand nothing. Interest in the idea is the basis of skill in the hand.

Methods.— Method is an orderly way of doing. In drawing, method should not be mistaken for the knowledge that enables one to draw. Simply knowing the method will not enable one to draw any more than a mere knowledge of notes will enable one to sing. The method is a tool to work with, the same as a pencil, only less material; it is the road but not the destination.

Holding the Pencil.— There is no particular position or prescribed rule for holding the pencil. No particular way is natural for all. Forget the pencil, forget the hand in the intensity of interest in the idea; and in the majority of cases there will be no need of correcting the hand. Cramped ideas are the cause of cramped hands. Liberate the idea and you liberate the expression of the idea. The general law governing the above and similar questions is this: *Place as little obstruction between the idea and its expression as possible.*

The Eraser.—Yes, let the pupil use the eraser, but teach him how to use it. It is a tool to work with just as much as the pencil, and has its place. Excessive erasing is caused by incomplete thought. The remedy is to make the thought which the line represents complete before it is drawn. If the habit is formed of marking out the work with light lines before finishing with heavier, then there will be little use of erasing at all. To break up the habit of excessive erasing you may at times take away the eraser, or require the pupil to ask permission to use it each time.

The Supremacy of the Child.—Type forms, objects, models, methods, and all the points and lines that go with them, are for the child, not the child for them. They are but tools to work with, aids in developing and unfolding the qualities of mind. The child should never be made subservient to these, for they exist solely for his purpose.

FIRST YEARS OF DRAWING.

The keynote of the first year of drawing should be *activity*. *Talk little and draw much* should be the motto.

Draw anything and everything that claims the child's interest. Place interest and the child's activity before the set plan.

If the drawing is taught to a class let it be short; five minutes, never more than ten, is long enough.

Let drawing on the blackboard predominate, as the large arm movements necessary on the blackboard are better adapted to small children. Encourage the endeavor — the *try* — rather than look for results.

The beginning in drawing is best made with the images the child has already formed in his mind, and then extended to more definite and concrete forms. As much as possible he should be guided into reproducing images from his own life and experience.

The following outline is not intended to *limit* but to suggest the lines of drawing that can profitably be followed in these grades.

The teacher must use her own judgment to a large extent, both as to the amount to be used and the order in which it is given.

GENERAL OUTLINE OF FIRST YEAR DRAWING.

Drawing from memory and the imagination.
Illustrating stories and bits of poetry.
Drawing representing action.
Drawing of trees.
Two-handed exercises.
Drawing in connection with number, language and nature work.
Color work.

General Outline of Second Year Drawing.

Drawing from memory and imagination.
Illustrating stories and bits of poetry.
Drawing representing action.
Two-handed exercises.
Place and relation of objects.
Relative size of objects.
Object drawing.
Study of a tree.
Study of a bird.
Study of an animal.
Water colors.

General Outline of Third Year Drawing.

Memory and imaginative drawing.
Illustrating language exercises.
Action drawing.
Two-handed exercises.
Teaching proportion.
Object drawing.
Unity in drawing.
Study of a tree.
Study of a bird.
Study of an animal
Water colors.

AUGSBURG'S DRAWING.

CHAPTER I.

DRAWING FROM MEMORY AND THE IMAGINATION.

THE BEGINNING in drawing should be made with images that the child has already formed in his mind and extended to more definite and concrete forms. He will reproduce best that which has appealed to him strongest. The following subjects are merely suggestive. They are to suggest to the teacher *sources* from which material may be drawn.

SUBJECTS FOR MEMORY DRAWING.

Draw the house you live in.
Draw the barn where the horse lives.
Draw the shed where the bossie cow stays.
Draw the coop where the chickens are kept.
Draw the kennel where Rover sleeps.
Draw for me some of the playthings you have.
Have you a wheelbarrow at home? Draw it for me.
Have you a hatchet? Show me how it looks.
Draw me a picture of dollie, Rover, Kittie, Bunnie, the bossie cow, etc.
Draw the corn popper, feather duster, mamma's broom, rolling-pin, papa's lantern, sister's fan, etc.
Let's draw all the different things used in the garden — rake, hoe, spade, shovel, pick, etc.
Let's draw the tools the carpenter uses — hammer, mallet, plane, ax, saw, etc.

Let's draw the tools used by the mason. Blacksmith. Shoemaker. Housekeeper, etc.

Draw for me the furniture in your room.

Draw a wagon, buggy, balloon, engine, car, trolley car, etc.

Did you ever see a scare-crow? If so, draw one.

If living near the water, draw a tug boat, schooner, sloop, ship, yacht, steamer, ferry boat, scow, skiff, canoe, anchor, etc.

Draw a hat, cap, rubber, slipper, etc.

Show me by means of a drawing where you caught the fish. Where you camped last summer. The boat in which you went rowing.

All children cannot draw all of these, but most children can draw some of them.

IMAGINATIVE DRAWING.

In the following exercises the post may be changed for any other object the teacher may choose, such as a stump, a log, a rock, or a box. The teacher may, if she wishes, show the children how to draw this first object, but no more. The post is merely intended for an object to start from.

(1) DRAW a post and on it place a ball; a basket; a bird's house; a Jack-o'-lantern; a cat; a squirrel; an owl.

(2) DRAW a post and to it hitch a kite; a boat; a horse; a goat; a dog; a cow.

(3) DRAW a post and place by the side of it a wheelbarrow; a cart; a rake; a pitchfork; three rabbits, a deer.

(4) DRAW a post and represent a boy sitting on it; standing on it; leaning on it; leaning against it; sitting against it; pushing against it; pulling it; hammering it; spearing it; throwing a stone at it; lassooing it.

ILLUSTRATING STORIES AND BITS OF POETRY.

These oral pictures and stories should be very direct, plain, short and undivided. The teacher's aim is to make the mental image as vivid and strong as possible. The words alone should form the mental image. *The teacher must not show the pupil how by means of a drawing.*

The following are some simple examples of stories and bits of poetry suitable to illustrate:

There is a boy sitting on a log. He is fishing.

I see a post standing alone. There is a cat on top of the post and a dog on the ground.

There is a tree. A boy is leaning against the tree. He is flying a kite.

I see a boy running and a little girl trying to catch him. The boy is running toward a tree.

There is a bird's house on top of a post. Two doves live in the house. One is on the roof, the other is flying away to get food for her little ones inside of the house.

Three wise men of Gotham
Went to sea in a bowl;
And if the bowl had been stronger,
My song had been longer.

Simple Simon went a-fishing
For to catch a whale;
And all the water he had got
Was in his mother's pail.

———

High on the branch of a walnut tree
A bright-eyed squirrel sat.
What was he thinking so earnestly?
And what was he looking at?

———

There come the little gentle birds,
Without a fear of ill,
Down to the murmuring water's edge,
And freely drink their fill.

———

Here we go to the branches high!
Here we come to the grasses low!
For the spiders and flowers and birds and I
Love to swing when the breezes blow.

———

Three little kittens slept on a mat,
Three little kittens white and fat;
And they were dreaming of milk and mice,
And everything that a cat thinks nice.

———

"Creak, creak, creak," the weather-cock growls,
"I think I am the most ill-used of fowls.
I never foretold bad weather yet
But you went in while I got wet;
Say what you may I don't think it's right
To keep me twisting from morning to night."

Three Trees.

The pine tree grew in the wood,
  Tapering straight and high;
Stately and proud it stood,
  Black-green against the sky.
Crowded so close it sought the blue,
And ever upward it reached and grew.

The oak tree stood in the field.
  Beneath it dozed the herds;
It gave to the mower a shield,
  It gave a home to the birds.
Sturdy and broad it guarded the farms
With its brawny trunk and knotted arms.

The apple tree grew by the wall,
  Ugly and crooked and black;
But it knew the gardener's call,
  And the children rode on its back.
It scattered its blossoms upon the air,
It covered the ground with fruitage fair,

Up the oak tree, close beside him,
Sprang the squirrel, Adjidaumo,
In and out among the branches,
Coughed and chattered from the oak tree,
Laughed, and said between his laughing,
"Do not shoot me, Hiawatha!"

And the rabbit from his pathway
Leaped aside, and at a distance
Sat erect upon his haunches,

Half in fear and half in frolic,
Saying to the little hunter,
"Do not shoot me, Hiawatha!"

Then, upon one knee uprising,
Hiawatha aimed an arrow;
Scarce a twig moved with his motion,
Scarce a leaf was stirred or rustled,
But the wary roebuck started,
Stamped with all his hoofs together,
Listened with one foot uplifted,
Leaped as if to meet the arrow;
Ah! the singing, fatal arrow,
Like a wasp it buzzed and stung him!

By the shores of Gitche Gumee,
By the shining Big-Sea-Water,
Stood the wigwam of Nokomis,
Daughter of the Moon, Nokomis.
Dark behind it rose the forest,
Rose the black and gloomy pine trees,
Rose the firs with cones upon them;
Bright before it beat the water,
Beat the clear and sunny water.

At the door on summer evenings
Sat the little Hiawatha;
Heard the whispering of the pine trees,
Heard the lapping of the water,
Sounds of music, words of wonder.

CHAPTER II.

Action Drawing.

Life.—Dear to every child's heart is life, the vital element of action, and the vital element of a drawing. If this element is lacking the drawing is uninteresting, however carefully it may be drawn. Action expresses life. It is usually one of the first aims of the draughtsman " to get the action right," *i.e.*, to express by means of lines the exact movement that will make the thought plain.

Of the three elements of drawing, *form, color,* and *action,* children love *action* best. Form is of very little interest to them unless coupled with *use* that lends interest to the form, but action that expresses life is always interesting.

Action Figures.—These action figures have been reduced to the most simple form possible. All details that can be dispensed with have been discarded, leaving only the essential features; and these, as far as possible, are indicated by a single line.

To further simplify the proportions of the figures, the body, thigh and leg may be made of equal length. The body may be represented by a single line or by an elliptical mass, as in Figs. 19–22.

The difference between a child and a grown person is shown in the proportion of the head to the rest of the body. The larger the head in proportion to the body and limbs the smaller the child, as shown in Figs. 23–26.

Direction of Line.—It is the chief function of the line to *indicate direction*. The direction is of far more importance than the quality of the line. It is the correctness of this direction and the proportion that expresses the action — that makes the thought visible.

Order of Teaching Action Drawing.— Proceed in the teaching of action drawing in the following order:
1. *By Imitation or Copying.*
2. *By Imagination and Memory.*
3. *By Perception and Direct Observation.*

Children must learn *how* to represent action before much progress can be made in expressing it. The child can hardly do this by direct observation. Even the slowest movements of an animate form are confusing to the average pupil. The best way is, first, to learn the action through the copy, and gain power by practice in expressing the action; then use it in imaginative and memory work, and lastly, use direct observation to verify, correct and perfect the representation of action already gained.

Teaching Action Drawing by Copy.—The following are excellent methods of teaching action drawing by means of the copy.

Draw on the blackboard, just above the reach of the pupils, a row of action figures, say Figs. 1–17, and let the pupils systematically copy them for the purpose of learning how to represent the action.

Another way is to paste hectograph copies of these action figures on pieces of cardboard, $3\frac{1}{2}$ x 5 inches, similar to Fig. 40, and give them to the pupils to copy.

Sets of cards similar to Fig. 40, representing action, may be procured, in which the actions are arranged systematically ready for the pupils to copy. This copying is not mere busy work, but is for a purpose. The aim is to learn how to represent action in very much the same manner as one learns a piece of prose or poetry.

Imagination and Memory Work.—When the correct representation of a certain action has been learned it should be used in some imaginative way in connection with either a story, language lesson or drawing

After the pupils have learned through copying how to draw action figures, choose some game they are acquainted with and let them illustrate it by means of action figures; for example, a game of ball. Write on the blackboard an action of the human figure common in ball playing, such as catching, throwing, knocking, tossing, running, and have the pupils represent it by means of an action drawing. Let those who have succeeded place their drawings on the blackboard.

Draw a post on the blackboard and ask the pupils to draw it and place an action figure :

>Standing on the post.
>Sitting on the post.
>Pushing against the post.
>Leaning on the post.
>Pulling at the post.
>Climbing on the post.
>Sitting against the post.
>Jumping over the post.
>Standing at the right of the post.

The following actions are also suitable for imaginative drawing:

>A boy jumping over a hay-cock.

A boy climbing a pole.
A boy rolling a hoop.
A boy swinging.
Two boys playing horse.
Two boys pulling a rope.

In your drawing lessons always take advantage of games in their season, such as representations of flying kites, playing marbles, ball, jumping the rope, skating, snow-balling, etc.

When the circus or similar events come to town, take advantage of them, and have a drawing lesson based on that which interests the children.

Direct Observation. — Give out an action for the pupils to study, such as walking, running or jumping, and ask the pupils to observe the position of the body, arms, feet and legs in these actions. Let a boy walk or jump before the class that they may observe the action more closely, and then let them represent it as nearly as possible on their tablets. Let those who have been most successful in representing these actions place them on the blackboard for the benefit of all.

Ask a pupil to climb upon a box or similar object, and jump off, then let the pupils represent the action as near as possible. This may be repeated.

Tell a pupil to stand on the platform and throw a light rubber ball, or wad of paper, and let the pupils represent the action of throwing by a drawing on their tablets.

Ask a boy to stand on a box or platform and "pose," that is, take a familiar position, such as catching a ball, and let the pupils represent it by an action drawing. Other poses:

Shooting with a gun.
Shooting with a bow.
Throwing a spear.

Pushing, pulling a rope, sitting, and like actions can also be represented in poses.

In all of this work draw *with* the pupils to show them *how*. Lead the way. It is not necessary or desirable that they should copy your drawing, even if you place it on the blackboard.

Though all may be making drawings at the same time it is not difficult to teach the pupils to be self-reliant and to depend on their own efforts. This may be done by speaking deprecatingly, but in a kindly manner, of those drawings that are copies of he one the teacher has drawn on the blackboard. Teach the

28   AUGSBURG'S DRAWING.

pupils to rely on their own mental image, rather than take the mental image of another. All may use the same idea, the same principle, the same method, but each should represent the idea,

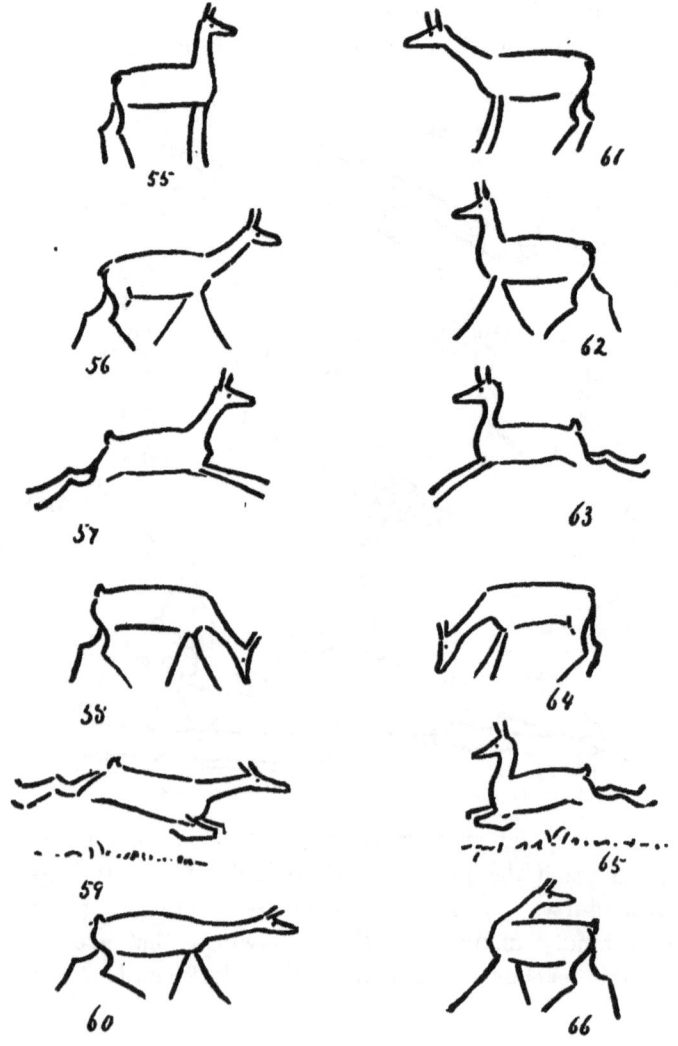

use the principle, and employ the method in his own way, and as independently as possible.

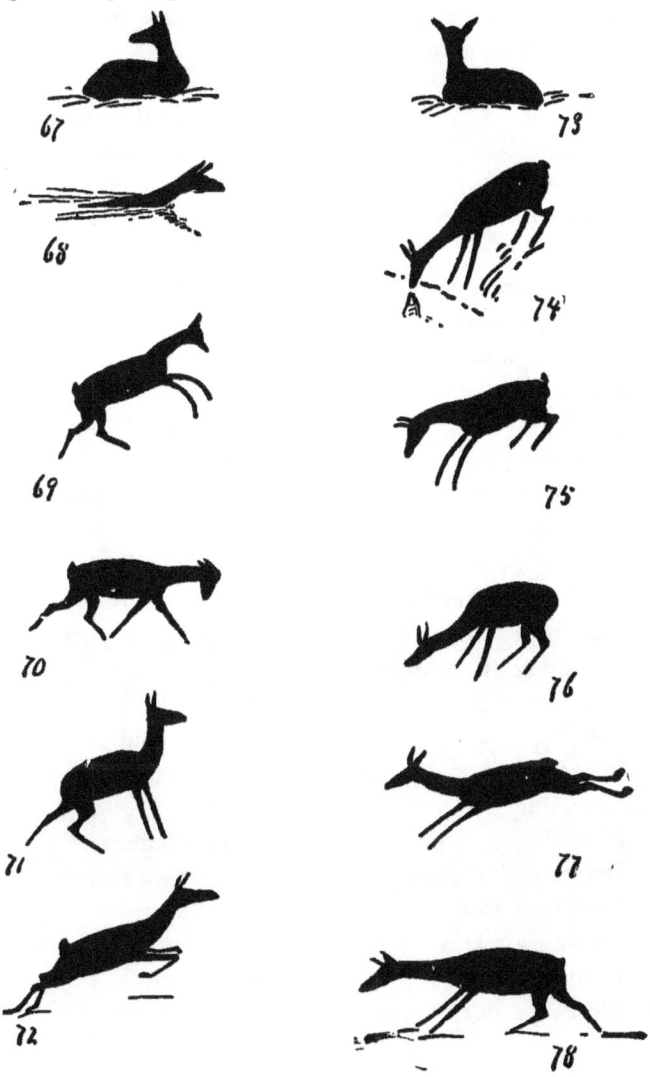

AUGSBURG'S DRAWING.

Subjects for Action Drawing.—Children can only represent those actions with which they are acquainted. The following actions most children are familiar with and can represent if they have been taught how to represent action.

Walking	Jumping the rope
Running	Playing marbles
Jumping	Shooting a gun
Dancing	Shooting a bow
Climbing	Throwing a spear
Playing horse	Rolling a hoop
Rowing a boat	Riding a bicycle
Paddling a canoe	Pulling a rope
Playing tag	Pushing
Fishing	Flying a kite
Swimming	Coasting
Swinging	Climbing a ladder
Skating	Carrying a pail
Keeling over	Carrying a rock
Walking on hands	Carrying a basket
Turning a somersault	Carrying a post
Wheeling a wheelbarrow	log
	Picking up
Spading	Sowing seed
Pitching hay	Mowing hay
Shoveling	Hoeing
Pounding	Crying papers
Drawing a wagon	Carrying a hoe
Pushing a cart	Driving
Playing a piano	Speaking a piece
Beating a drum	Tug of war
Blowing a horn	Falling down

The Action Principle the Same in Most Animals.

The action of animals is in principle very much the same. For example, the running of the deer, horse, cow, dog, rat, etc., are the same in principle, but differ in details and the characteristics of the animal. Observe in Figs. 79–86 that the position of the legs is the same in each figure. It is not necessary to learn the action of each animal separately, if the action of one animal is learned, it becomes the basis of the action of all other animals.

Almost any animal may be chosen as a type for the study of action, but perhaps the deer is the best for general purposes; the body is simple in form, the legs long and slender, and the head and neck easy to represent.

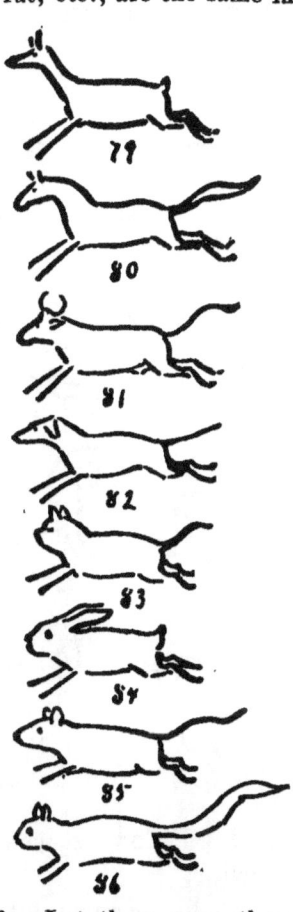

The manner of studying an animal is the same as in the study of the action figures:

First — Learn the action through the copy.

Second — Use the action in imaginative and memory work.

Third — Perfect the action by direct observation.

1. For example, let the pupils copy the action of the deer, Figs. 55–66. Let them copy these figures systematically until they can represent an action with some degree of accuracy.

2. Use the action in connection with a story or a picture. Draw a hay-cock on the blackboard and ask the pupils to represent a deer jumping over it; lying to the right of it; to the left; in front of it, etc.

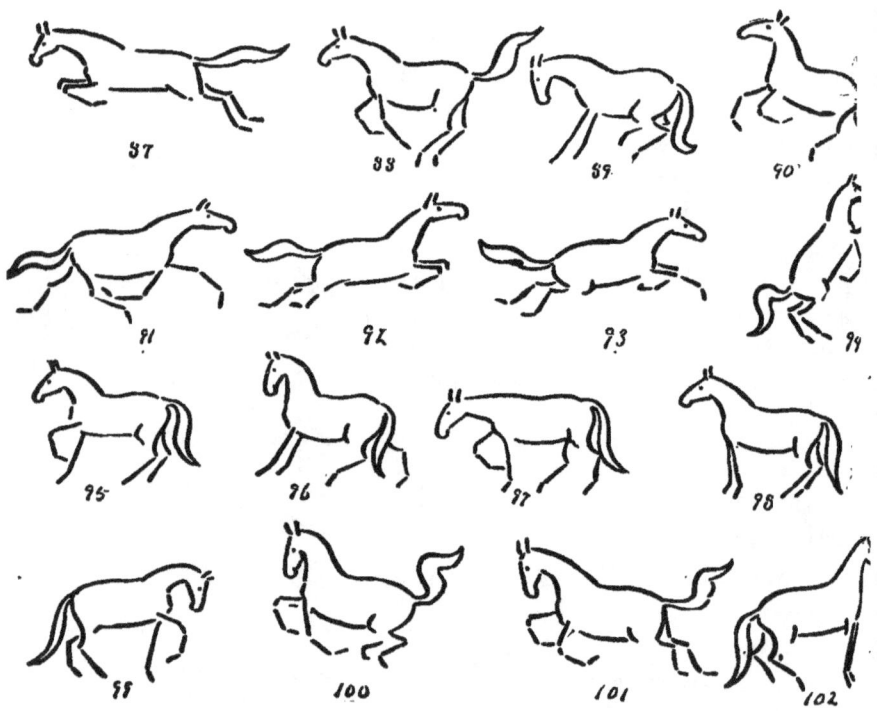

3. Follow up where possible with the study of the real animal.

In like manner take up the study of the horse, dog, and squirrel, observing the real animal to correct, verify, and perfect the action. A squirrel can be brought into the school-room for study and observation.

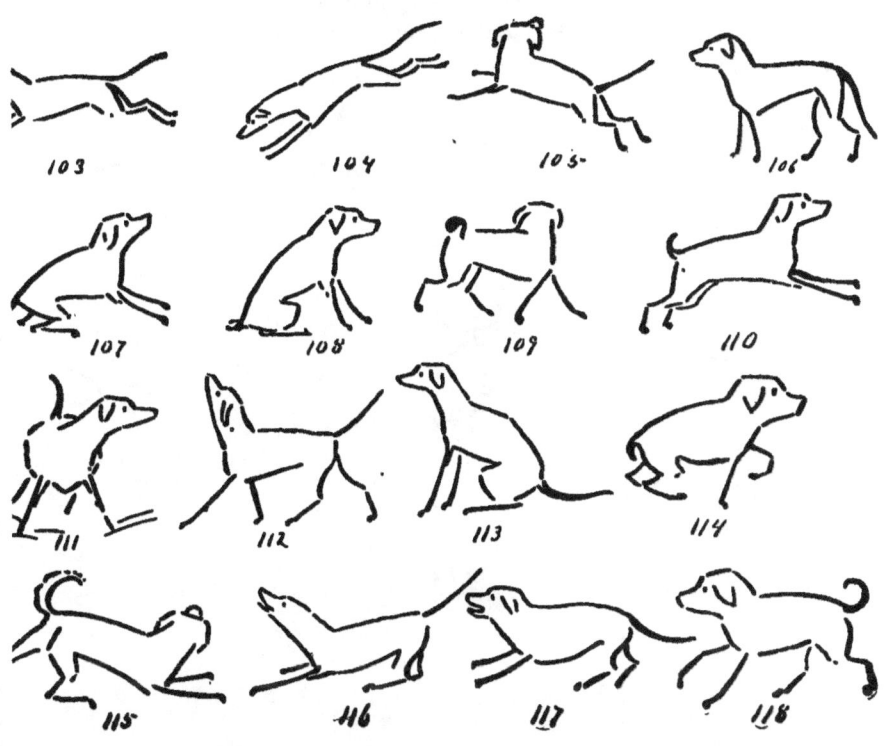

34   AUGSBURG'S DRAWING.

The same general plan is followed in the study of the action of birds. Fig. 119 represents the principle actions in flying.

Action cards containing the principle actions of the deer, horse, dog and birds arranged systematically may be procured or these actions may be copied and by means of the hectograph be given to each pupil.

CHAPTER III.

Ambidextrous or Two-Handed Drawing.

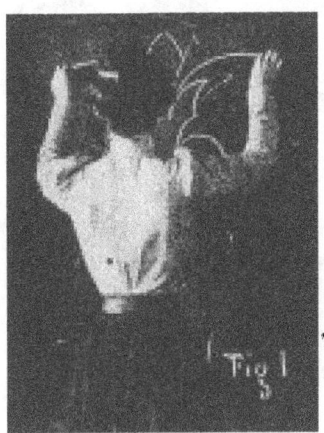

Fig. 3

Ambidextrous Drawing is an exercise adapted to large free arm movements, symmetrical and preferably decorative in character. Its aim is as follows:

To co-ordinate the two hands so they will work together freely and harmoniously.

To develop *skill, freedom,* and *speed* which can be done more rapidly and easily by using both hands together than either separately.

This work, especially in the primary grades, is adapted to the blackboard only.

Skill Universal in Its Application.— It is generally recognized that skill acquired in one line of work, is more or less utilized in all other lines. A skilled carpenter would not make a clumsy machinist, nor would a skilled wood-carver leave his cunning behind if employed in a blacksmith shop. Skill acquired in any line of industry is not lost when applied in other lines. Skill acquired in drawing when the pupil is at school will be utilized in the carpenter, machine, and blacksmith shops; in the millinery, dress-making and embroidery establishments; in the dentist office or engine room.

36   AUGSBURG'S DRAWING.

If skill is universal in its application, it is well to **extend its usefulness**, and make it as broad as the wants of man. This can be done in no better way than by teaching the ambidextrous use of the hands. By doing this, energy may be conserved and the amount of work done in a given time increased. It is not intended

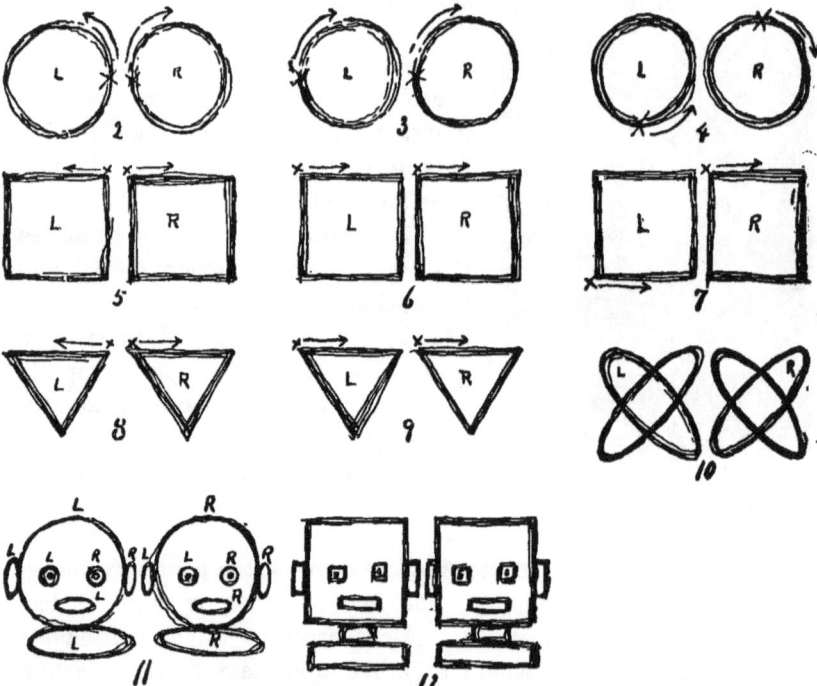

in this two-handed drill to require the left hand to do the work of the right. This would practically be impossible. The aim is to make the hands mutually helpful.

Figs. 1–12 are *co-ordinating exercises* and are made with *both hands working together*. R stands for right and L for left, indicating the part each hand is to perform. The x indicates the starting point, and the ---- > the direction that the hand travels. *All of these exercises may be reversed.*

Each exercise should be abandoned soon after it has become automatic. The co-ordinating exercises may be practised by the pupils on the tops of their desks, using the forefinger in place of the crayon.

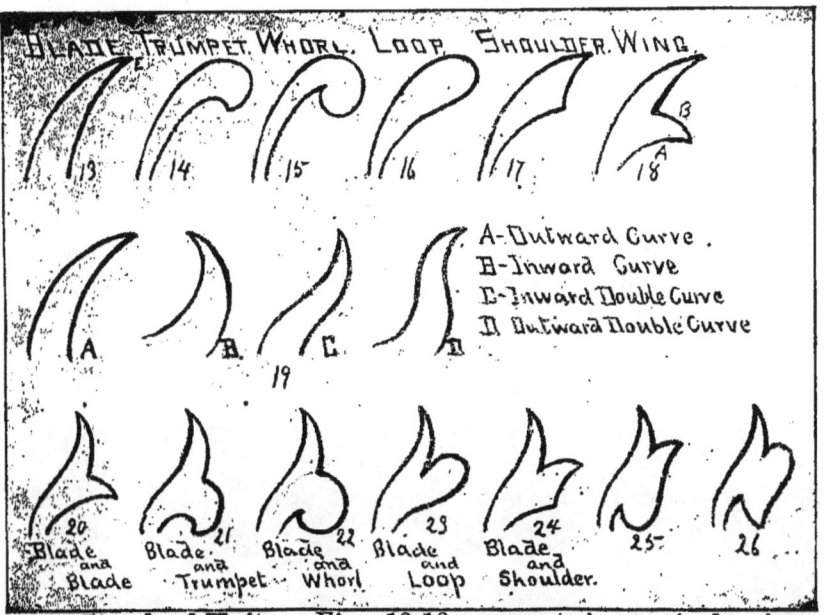

Standard Units.—Figs. 13-18 represent six standard units. These units contain the principle elements found in historic ornament and in modern decoration and design. These units are of so much importance and are so foundational in character that they should be thoroughly learned and memorized.

The standard units are very similar.

Carry the point *E* of the *blade* around further and the *trumpet*

38   AUGSBURG'S DRAWING.

is formed; carry it still further and the *whorl* is formed; eliminate the point entirely and the *loop* is formed; add another point and the *shoulder* is formed. The *wing* is a compound unit made by uniting the blade with itself.

Fig. 19 represents the four kinds of curves that may be used with nearly all units.

A represents the *outward curve*, *B* the *inward curve*, *C* the *inward double curve*, and *D* the *outward double curve*.

Figs. 20-26 represent the principal *wing* units. The wing units are formed by uniting the *blade* with each of the standards. Thus: Fig. 20 is formed by uniting the *bläde* with *itself*. Fig. 21, by uniting the *blade* and *trumpet*, Fig. 22, the *blade* and *whorl*, Fig. 23, the *blade* and the *loop*, and Fig. 24, the *blade* and *shoulder*. Fig. 25 is formed by changing the line *A* of the *wing* to the outward double curve, and Fig. 26, by changing line *B*.

Figs. 27-32 represent the standard units doubled. These are suitable and adapted to two-handed exercises.

Figs. 33-39 represent the wing units, Figs. 20-26, doubled.

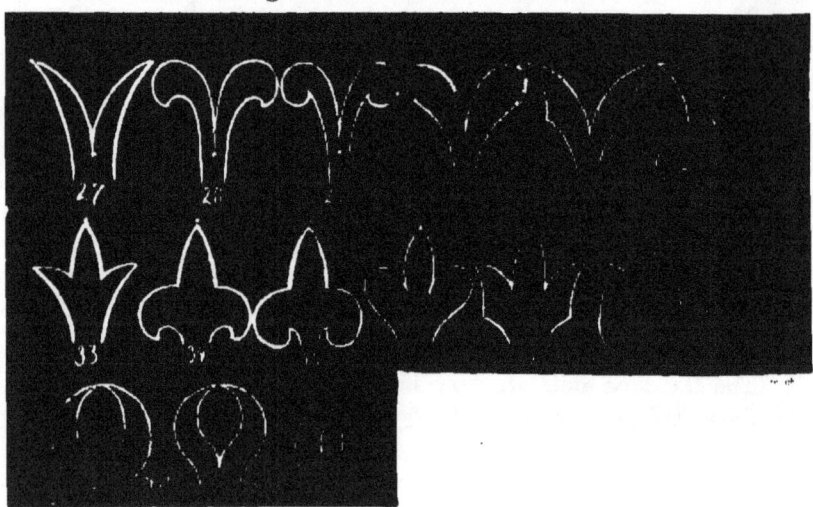

AUGSBURG'S DRAWING.

Figs. 27–32 are in outward curve. They may be drawn in *inward curve* similar to Fig. 40 or in *inward double curve* as shown in Fig. 41, or in *outward double curve* as shown in Fig. 42.

The *x* in the above drawings shows the beginning point when drawing with both hands.

The drawing of these designs on the blackboard is very rapid work. A class can readily draw a set similar to Figs. 27–32 in less than five minutes after they have memorized the units.

Figs. 43–47 represent a very serviceable series of units for

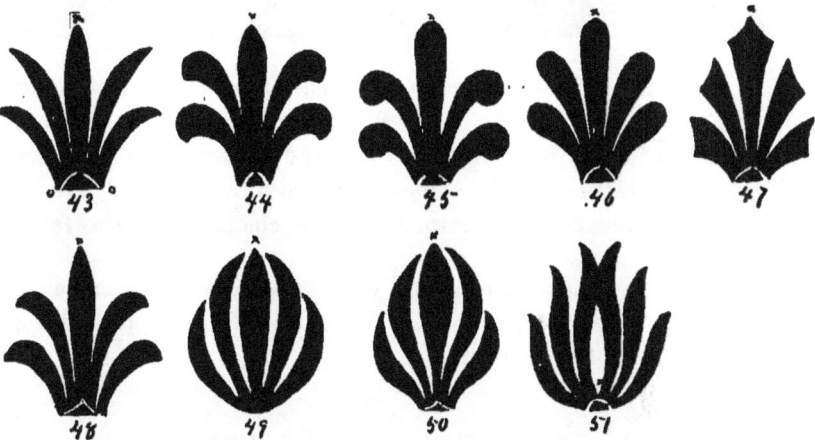

two-handed exercises. They are based on the standard units Fig. 43 is the *blade*, Fig. 44 the *trumpet*, Fig. 45 the *whorl*, Fig. 46 the *loop*, and Fig. 47 the *shoulder*. All of these are drawn in *outward curves*.

Fig. 48 is drawn in *outward curve*, Fig. 49 in *inward curve*, Fig. 50 in *inward double curve*, and Fig. 51 in *outward double curve*. Each of the standard units may be drawn in the same manner.

The Scroll. — The *double curve*, Fig. 52, is considered the most beautiful of lines, and the combination of the *single* and *double*

curve, Fig. 53, the most beautiful combination of lines. This union of the single and double curve is, perhaps, the most common combination found in decorative work, and *is one of the important elements to be learned*. The elements of the scroll, Fig. 54, are the single and double curve combined. These elements are also found in the double curved units.

Fig. 55 represents the scroll with *outward curving* branches, and Fig. 56, with *inward curving* branches. These represent the principal forms of the scroll.

AUGSBURG'S DRAWING. 41

Figs. 57-63 represent some additional forms of the scroll that are serviceable as main lines in forming designs.

To draw with ease and facility the curves of the scroll requires a great deal of practice and much persistent effort, but the gain to the pupil in skill and grace will richly repay all the work that may be put forth in the mastery of these elements.

These scrolls may be made with both hands *together* or with both hands *alternating.* For example, in Fig. 61, the part at the

left may be made with the left hand, and then the part at the right with the right hand, or both parts may be drawn together.

The scroll, Fig. 54, and similar figures may be drawn double, the part to the left drawn with the left hand and the part to the right with the right hand. Always draw first with the left hand and then repeat with the right.

All symmetrical objects can be drawn with two hands, and the power to go further increases wonderfully with practice.

Vase forms, similar to Figs. 64–68, are well adapted to this kind of drawing, as well as many other forms of china and earthen ware.

Figs. 69–80 represent another phase of this work. These drawings are more interesting to children than those of a decorative character, but are less valuable for training purposes. These drawings should be used more in the nature of a device to add humor, variety and interest to the work.

Preparing for Two-Handed Drawing. — The aims are: To gain skill, freedom, and speed in the use of the hands; to co-

ordinate the two hands so they will work easily and freely together to learn some of the fundamental elements of Decorative Design. To do this, facility should be placed before accuracy. Out of facility will grow accuracy, *providing the idea grows also.* It is the endency of the idea to perfect itself through repetition, providing the hand and mind work together. If there is interest, there is growth, but there is little or no progress when the mind is in a passive state and the perfecting element dormant. Quantity will not lead to quality unless there is a striving for perfection. To give the idea a chance to grow and perfect itself, ambidextrous exercises should be repeated each day for one week. *These exercises should not be more than five minutes long.*

The two-handed work should be divided into groups of what can be drawn in about five minutes, working under favorable conditions and then work to fulfill these conditions.

The standard units, Figs. 13–18, should be learned by the pupil at his seat, by carefully copying them until they can be reproduced from memory.

If desired, the co-ordinating exercises, Figs. 1–12, may be practised on top of the desk, using the finger in place of the crayon.

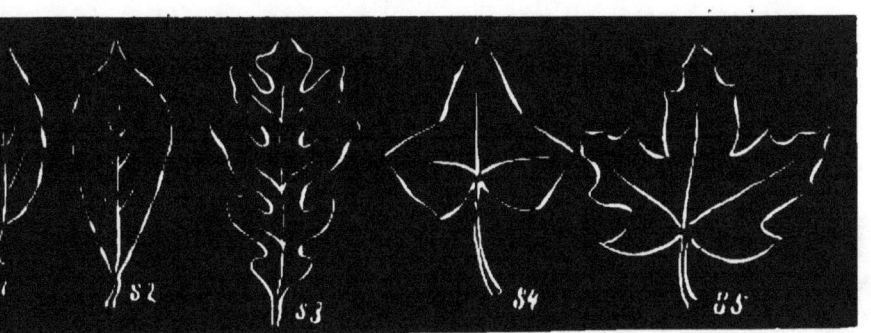

MANNER OF CONDUCTING A CLASS IN TWO-HANDED DRAWING.

Divide the pupils into divisions that can comfortably work at the blackboards, allowing two feet of space for each pupil. Each pupil should have his own place permanently. Each place should be supplied with crayon and one eraser.

The leader, which may be either the teacher or a pupil, should stand at the blackboard where all can see his work plainly.

The leader uses three commands: *Look. Draw. Erase.* At the command "Look," all pupils look at the leader while he draws, say Fig. 27. Then at the command "Draw," all draw Fig. 27 the same as the leader did.

At the command "Erase," all erase their work ready for the next number in the group.

The number of drawings that a class can draw in a given time depends largely on the alertness and decision of the leader.

AUGSBURG'S DRAWING.

PERFECTING EXERCISES are for the special purpose of raising the standard of excellerce, correcting mannerisms, and perfecting the ideal. For example, all may be able to draw *the trumpet*, Fig. 14, but very imperfectly. Then a perfecting exercise would have for its object the perfecting of this unit; learning how to draw it more perfectly, making it more beautiful, and raising the ideal higher.

The manner of conducting a perfecting lesson is by comparison. The leader places on the blackboard the element, say the trumpet, and all try to make a similar one, copying it again and again and receiving such help and suggestions as the leader can give.

CHALK DUST in the room is caused (1) by quick erasing, (2) by the upward stroke of the eraser. The remedy is to *erase slowly, downward*. There is no excuse for clouds of dust in the class-room if the teacher cares to stop it.

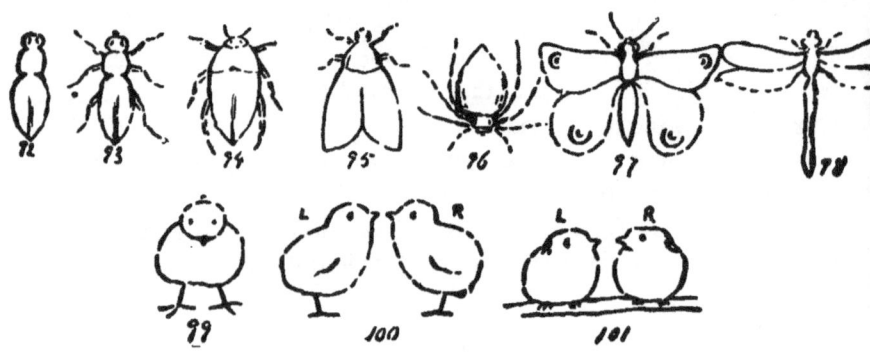

AUGSBURG'S DRAWING

FIVE-MINUTE DRILL EXERCISES ARRANGED IN GROUPS.

Group 1.— Figs. 2, 3, 4, 27, 28, 29, 30, 31, 69, 70 and 71.

Group 2.— Figs. 27, 28, 29, 30 and 31 in inward curve, similar to Fig. 40, also Fig. 72.

Group 3.— Figs. 27, 28, 29, 30, and 31 in inward double curve, similar to Fig. 41, also Fig. 73.

Group 4.— Figs. 27, 28, 29, 30 and 31 in outward double curve, similar to Fig. 42.

Learn the wing units, Figs. 20–26. Commit them to memory so that they are known as well as the letters of the alphabet.

Group 5.— Figs. 5, 6, 7, 33, 34, 35, 36, 37, 38, 39 and 74.

Group 6.— Figs. 33, 34, 35, 36, 37, 38, 39, divided by outward curves as Fig. 102, also Figs. 75 and 76.

Group 7.— Figs. 33, 34, 35, 36, 37, 38, and 39, divided by inward curves as in Fig. 103, also Figs. 77 and 78.

Group 8.— Figs. 33, 34, 35, 36, 37, 38, and 39, divided by inward double curves, as in Fig. 104. Also Figs. 79 and 80.

Group 9.— Figs. 33, 34, 35, 36, 37, 38 and 39, divided by outward double curves, as in Fig. 105. Also Figs. 81, 82, and 83.

Group 10.— Figs. 8, 9, 43, 44, 45, 46, 47, 84 and 85.

Group 11.— Fig. 10. Figs. 43, 44, 45, 46 and 47 in inward curve, similar to Fig. 49. Also Figs. 36 and 37.

Group 12.— Figs. 43, 44, 45, 46 and 47 in inward double curve, similar to Fig. 50. Also Figs. 88 and 89.

Group 13.— Figs. 43, 44, 45, 46 and 47 in outward double curve, similar to Fig. 51.

Memorize Figs. 54, 55 and 56, as the foundational elements of the scroll.

Group 14.— Figs. 57, 58, 59, 60, 90 and 91.
Group 15.— Figs. 61, 62, 63, 92, 93, and 94.
Group 16.— Figs. 64, 65, 66, 67, 68, 95 and 96.

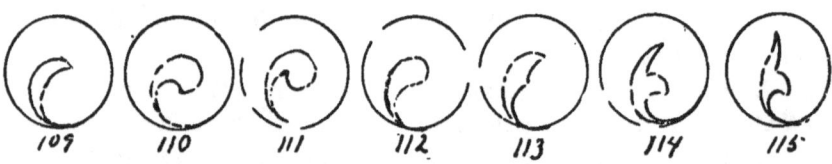

Group 17.— Draw Figs. 57, 59, 60, 61, 62, and 63, and to each scroll ending add a standard unit, as in Figs. 109–114.

Group 18.— Draw Fig. 106 and substitute in place of the blade the other standard units. Draw Figs. 97 and 98.

Group 19.— Draw Fig. 107 and substitute in place of the blade each of the other standard units. Draw also Figs. 99 and 100.

Any number of groups may be made by substituting in place of the shoulder and whorl of Fig. 108 the various standard units and the wings.

CHAPTER IV.

PLACE AND RELATION OF OBJECTS.

Drawing, from the very beginning, deals with the placing of one object, or a part of an object, in proportion to and relation with another object or part of an object. If we draw a bird, we must draw the head, body and tail in right proportion and relation to each other, or, if we wish to draw two apples or three balls, the same rule applies. And when we advance to still higher levels, we are only dealing with groups of objects and things, groups of animals, groups of men and women, forms of hills, dales, trees and plains, all of which must bear this relationship and proportion.

Material.— Spherical objects are the best to commence with, such as balls, apples, oranges, walnuts, cherries, plums and similar forms, though the principle is the same for all objects. Much better work can be done when each child has three round objects for his individual use, but good work can be done with only three or four large round objects placed on a table where all the class can see them.

Models and Drawings.—We get from the model the idea, from the drawing how to represent the idea on a flat surface.

The model is *the source*, the drawing, *the how*.

In the drawing we *perceive the principle* and to the model or object *apply the principle*.

From the drawing we *learn the method*, and then use it to *represent the model*.

The drawing shows *how to represent the model*, the model *verifies the drawing.*

The use of the model is to *form and correct* the mental image that of the drawing *to show how to make a picture* of this mental image.

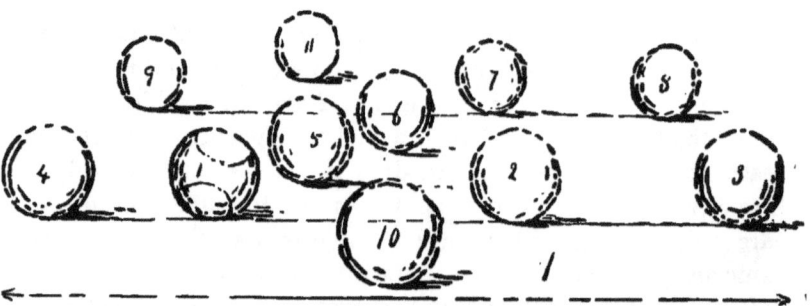

General Principles.— In Fig. 1 ball 2 is at the right of ball 1, because they rest on the same horizontal line.

Balls 2 and 3 are at the right, and ball 4 is at the left of ball 1.

Balls 1, 2, 3 and 4 are the same distance away.

Objects on the same horizontal line are the same distance away.

Ball 5 is farther away than ball 1, because it rests higher in the picture or drawing.

Ball 10 is nearer than ball 1, because it rests lower in the picture.

The farther away the object the higher it rests in the picture, and the nearer the object, the lower it rests in the picture.

(NOTE.— This is true only below the level of the eye and on a flat surface.)

Ball 10 is nearest and ball 11 farthest away. Ball 10 is lowest down and ball 11 highest up in the picture.

Balls 7, 8 and 9 are the same distance away.

AUGSBURG'S DRAWING.

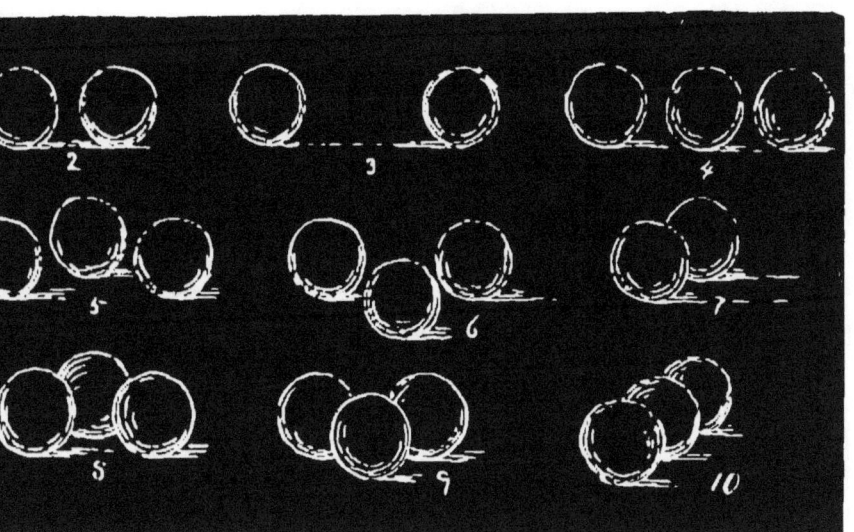

Methods. — The following are some of the most simple methods of teaching this subject.

Draw on the blackboard, say Fig. 2, and ask the pupils to place balls in the same position on their desks.

Ask a pupil to come to the table and place the balls on the table in the same position as the balls in the drawing. In like manner draw balls in various positions as suggested by Figs. 2-10, and let the pupils place balls in the same position on their desks or the table.

Place the balls in the position of Fig. 2 where all the pupils can see them plainly. The chalk rail is an excellent place.

Ask a pupil to go to the blackboard and draw the balls as you have placed them.

Ask the class to draw the balls on their tablets in the same position.

In like manner draw the various positions as suggested by Figs. 2–10.

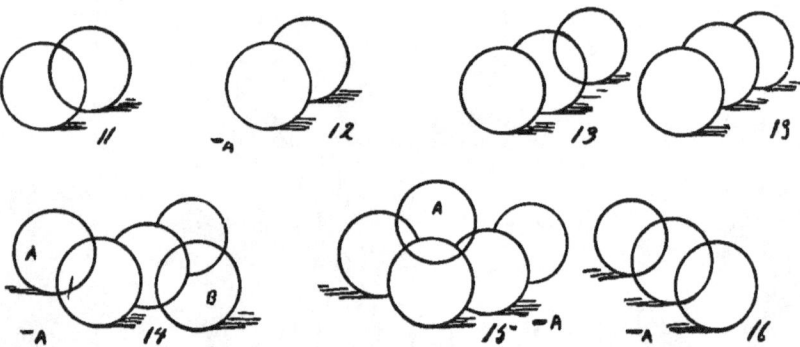

Draw on the blackboard Fig. 11 and erase that portion of the line of the second ball that cannot be seen so that it will look like Fig. 12. *This is to show the pupils how.* Now place Fig. 11 again on the blackboard and ask a pupil to come up and erase the right line, so it will look like Fig. 12. Add another ball as in Fig. 13, and ask a pupil to erase the line that could not be seen, so it will look like the next figure.

Add to Fig. 13 ball A as in Fig. 14, and have the unseen line erased. Add ball B and have the unseen lines erased. Add ball A to Fig. 15 and have the unseen line erased.

Place Fig. 16 on the blackboard and have the unseen lines erased. Do this until the pupils can recognize without hesitancy, the lines that should not show in the drawing.

Size of Object. — The farther away the object the smaller it appears, and of course, the smaller it is represented in the drawing. This may be shown to pupils in the following way : With your pencil measure, by sighting, various objects in the room and let the children see you do it. This is to *show them how.* Stand before the class and ask them to measure the length of your head, by sighting, with their pencil as a measure. After they have learned to do this, walk backward away from the class, and again ask them to measure your head in the same way. It will now measure less — will appear smaller. Reverse the process and the head appears to grow larger. (See chapter VI. book II.)

Compare the length of various objects in the room by thus measuring them with the pencil. Compare the length of objects out of doors — houses, trees, poles, etc.

Place two balls on the table in the position of balls 10 and 11 in Fig. 1, and have the pupils measure the nearer one and compare it with the one farther away.

Placing Objects. — Fig. 17 represents an apple with several marks around it. Each mark is numbered.

This drawing is used as follows: Draw an apple on the blackboard similar to Fig. 17. Place a mark, say mark 2, at the left of it, and ask the pupils to draw a similar apple on their tablets and place another apple like it in the position of mark 2. In like manner have them place apples on the other points.

Place two apples on the table as in Fig. 18. Draw the one with the stem on the blackboard. Ask a pupil to stand in front of the real apples and observe them closely and then step to the board and draw the other apple at the right distance, in the right position, and of the right size, as compared with the apple already drawn on the board. Let the other pupils judge whether it is drawn correctly. The character of the apple need not be required in this work, merely the size, distance, and position in regard to the apple already drawn. Perhaps repeated attempts of several pupils will be required before the apple is placed properly.

After the apples have been placed on the board properly erase them and ask all of the pupils to draw the apples as they are placed on the table. If Fig. 18 is too difficult, place three apples on the

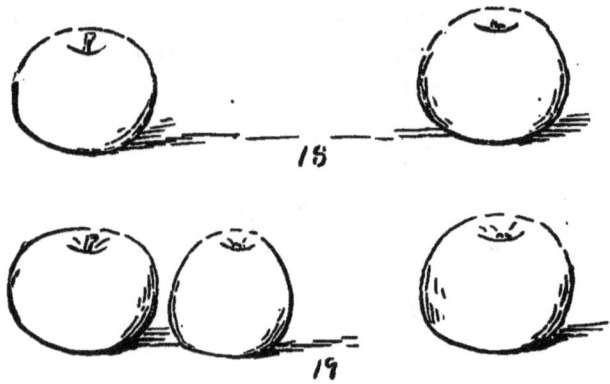

table as in Fig. 19, and draw the right and left apples and ask a pupil to draw the middle one, of the right size and in the right place.

After the pupils can place objects right and left of a given object, then positions similar to Figs. 5–10 may be given.

Draw an apple or similar object on the blackboard. See Fig. 17. Give the apple to a pupil and tell him to hold it in his hand so that it will look as represented in the drawing. Tell him to point to the same places on the apple in his hand, that you point to in the drawing. Point to the stem, right edge, top edge, etc. Reverse this process.

Draw an apple, Fig. 17, or similar object, on the blackboard and ask the pupils to draw a similar one on their tablets and place another like it —

    At the right of it.
    At the left of it.
    Behind it.
    In front of it.
    Place two apples behind it.
    Place two apples in front of it.

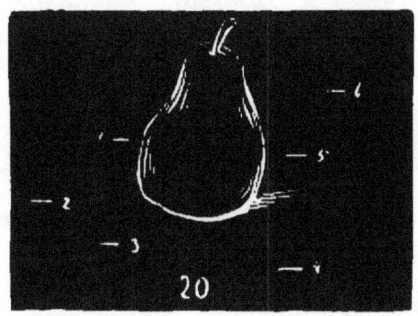

Draw a pear, Fig. 20, on the blackboard and ask the pupils to draw a similar one and place another like it on mark 1. On mark 2. On mark 3. On mark 4, etc.

Draw on the blackboard a box similar to Fig. 21, and ask the pupils to place an apple or similar object on top of it, on the right, left, or in front of it.

Draw a nest on the blackboard similar to Fig. 22. Ask the pupils to draw a similar one and place an egg in the nest. Two eggs. Three eggs. Place one inside and two outside of the nest, etc.

Devices.— Dear to every child's heart are life and action. There is no reason why these elements may not be introduced in this work. Care must, however, be taken not to let the device become primary and the principle you are teaching secondary. This may be guarded against by using the device only at the end of the lesson. The primary use of a device is that of an incentive;

rightly used, it may help to impress many of the highest truths in expression and method.

Figs. 23-26 are devices added to the object, and Figs. 27-31 represent the ball turned into some other object of similar form.

DRILL EXERCISES.

1. Draw Fig. 1 on the blackboard. John, you may take the pointer and point to ball 1. Point to a ball at the right of ball 1. At the left. Point to two balls at the right of ball 1.
Point to four balls the same distance away. To three balls the same distance away. To the nearest ball. The farthest ball. Which is the farthest away, ball 5 or 6? Why? Which is the nearest, ball 10 or 3? Why?

2. Draw Fig. 2 on the blackboard and have the pupils place two round objects in similar positions on their desks. Do the same with Fig. 3, Fig. 4, Fig. 5, Fig. 6, Fig. 7, Fig. 8, Fig. 9.

3. Place two balls on the chalk rail of the blackboard in the position of Fig. 2 and ask a pupil to draw them on the blackboard above the balls in the same position. Let the class criticise. Place the balls as in Fig. 3 and ask a pupil to do the same. Do the same with Fig. 4. The pupils may also draw these on their tablets.

4. Place three balls on a level surface such as a table. Ask a pupil to look at them carefully and draw the same on the blackboard. Do the same with Fig. 5, Fig. 6, Fig. 7, Fig. 8, Fig. 9, Fig. 10.

5. Draw Fig. 11 on the blackboard and ask a pupil to erase the *unseen* line so that one ball will appear behind the other. Add another ball as in Fig. 13. Add ball A as in Fig. 15. Add ball B as in Fig. 14. Add a ball to spot A in Fig. 12. Add a ball to spot A in Fig. 14. Add a ball to spot A in Fig. 15. Add a ball to spot A in Fig. 16.

6. Show pupils how to measure, by sighting, the length and width of objects with the lead pencil as a measure. Measure thus the length of a picture on the wall; the width of the picture. Measure the length of the teacher's head. Measure the length of her head while she advances; while she recedes. Compare the

length of a tree near by with a tree farther off. Compare the length of three telegraph poles. Compare the width of the pavement near by with the same farther away. Compare the diameter of two balls, one farther away than the other.

7. Draw an apple similar to Fig. 17 and place a similar apple on mark 2. On mark 1. On marks 1 and 2. On marks 3 and 6. On marks 4 and 1. On marks 1, 3, and 5.

8. Place two apples on the table similar to Fig. 18. Draw the one with the stem on the blackboard and have a pupil draw the other. Add a third apple as in Fig. 19 and have a pupil draw it on the blackboard.

9. Draw an apple on the blackboard and place another apple at the right of it and one at the left of it. One behind it. Two apples behind it. Two apples in front of it. Four apples around it.

10. Draw a pear similar to Fig. 20 and place a similar pear on mark 2. Place a pear on mark 1. Place a pear on mark 3. On mark 6. On marks 1 and 4. On marks 2, 3, and 5. On marks 2, 4, and 6.

11. Draw the front face of a box and on it place an apple. Place an apple to the right of it. To the left. Place an apple in front. Place two pears on top of the box. Place two balls in front of the box.

12. Draw a bird's nest and in it place one egg. Two eggs. Three eggs. Place two eggs in the nest and one egg on the outside. Place one egg inside and three eggs outside.

13. Draw a haycock and place another at the right of it. One at the left. Put the haycocks in the positions of Fig. 6. Fig. 7. Fig. 8. Fig. 9. Fig. 10.

The following chapter is a continuation of this subject. Trees are substituted in the place of round objects.

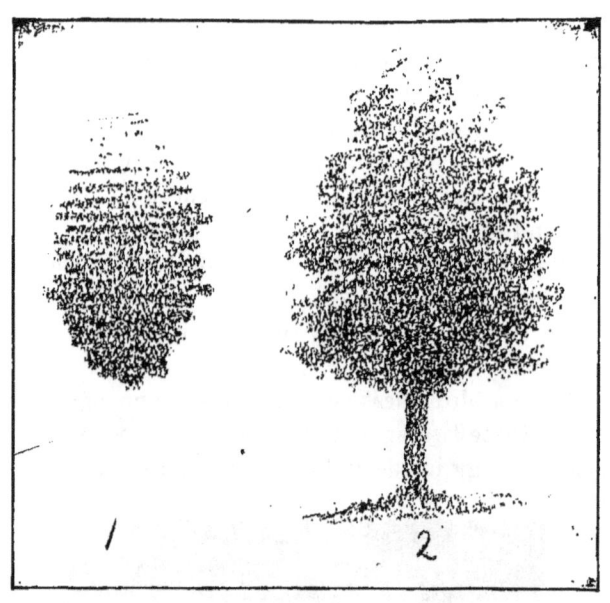

CHAPTER V.

THE DRAWING OF TREES.

The easiest and quickest way of representing trees is as follows :

With a soft pencil mark in the mass of the tree with a bold, free stroke, as in Fig. 1.

Then with a shorter stroke mark in the branches, softening the edges, and aiming to show the general character of the outline, as in Fig. 2.

Use the *end of the pencil* as in ordinary work, not the flat side. Work from the center outward.

The center of the tree is the trunk. *When making a drawing of trees the foliage and branches should spring from this trunk center outward and upward.* This is one of the most important laws of foliage representation, and should always be followed, or the unity of the tree will be destroyed and it will look like a heap of rubbish.

Do not attempt at first to vary the shade of the foliage. Put it on with one uniform shade, making trunk, limbs, and foliage about the same strength, similar to a shadow picture. *Aim to represent the form only.*

Blackboard Drawing.— Use the *side* of a *short* piece of crayon to represent the foliage.

Grasp the crayon with the first three fingers and thumb and then a broad or fine line can be made by merely tilting the crayon.

The method to be followed in drawing trees on the blackboard is the same as when using the pencil on paper, except that both the side and the end of the crayon are used.

Do not outline the trees before drawing them, but draw from within outward: aiming at the larger truths rather than the smaller ones. It is impossible to represent all the details; choose those which are essential to the tree as a whole and omit those of less importance.

The character of the branching is of more importance than exactness of outline, or the technical accuracy of the leaves. General character is one of the larger truths, and is usually lost if the lesser truths are observed too closely.

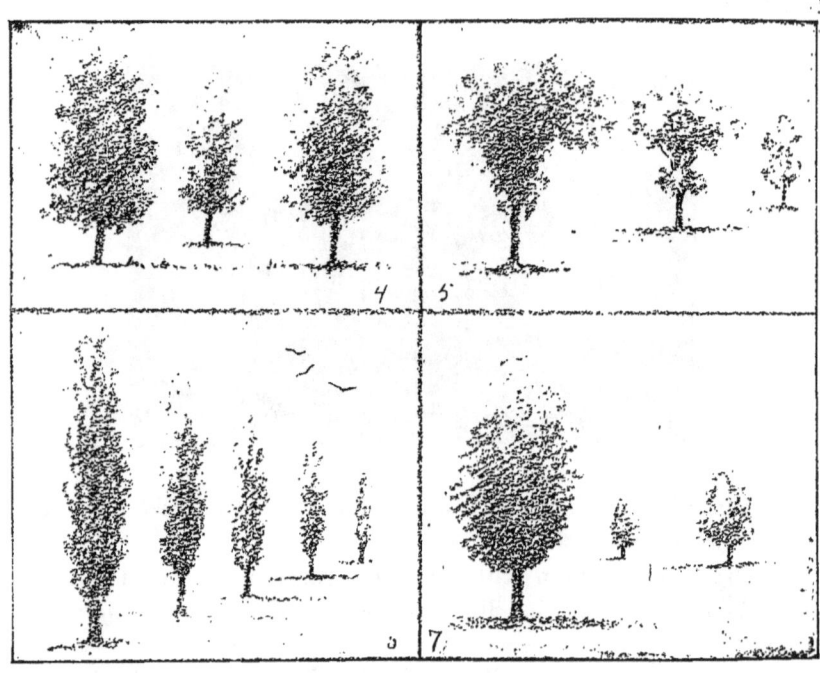

Placing of Trees.— Observe in Fig. 4 that the tree on the left and the one on the right are the same distance away, but the one in the middle is farther away. The mechanical method of placing an object farther away is to *place it higher in the picture.*

In Figs. 5, 6, and 7 the farther the trees are away the higher they are placed in the picture.

Trees are perhaps more often seen in mass of practically one shade, than in any other way. Trees between you and the light, trees seen through a haze or fog, trees seen on cloudy or dark days, and distant trees, are usually of one even shade, similar to those in Figs. 4–11. It is an excellent plan to teach pupils to reproduce trees in the mass as they appear in silhouette against the sky, especially when the trees are between them and the light.

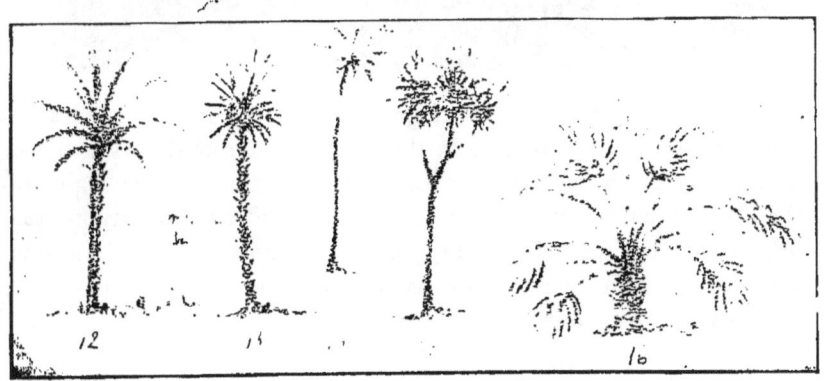

Figs. 12-15 represent several palm trees. They are drawn as follows: Make a small mass of uniform shade at the top of the trunk and from this draw the leaves or branches, being careful to make the leaves spring from the center or stem. The blackboard drawing, Fig. 3, is drawn in the same manner. Draw a light mass with the side of the crayon and then add the details with the end of the crayon.

There are many kinds of grasses, flowers, sprays of leaves that can be best represented in the same manner as the palm trees. The sprays of the pepper tree and umbrella plant on the right, in the above illustration, are made with the end of the crayon, the others with the side of the crayon, and the details marked in with the end of the crayon. This is a rapid and effective means of representing both flowers and leaves on the blackboard.

AUGSBURG'S DRAWING.

DRILL EXERCISES.

1. Show the class how to represent trees in the mass, as in Figs. 1 and 2.
2. Draw a tree and place another at the right of it.
3. Draw a tree and place another at the left of it.
4. Draw a tree and place another tree beyond it.

5. Draw a row of three trees extending away and to the right. See Fig. 5.
6. Draw a row of three trees extending away and to the left.
7. Draw a row of five trees extending away and to the right. See Fig. 6.
8. Draw a row of five trees extending away and to the left.

9. Draw a tree and represent two trees quite a long distance beyond it. See Fig. 7.
10. Draw a row of eucalyptus trees, Fig. 8, extending away and to the left.

11. Draw six oak trees similar to Figs. 9 and 10 various distances away.

12. Draw a row of six palm trees similar to Fig. 12, extending away and to the left.

13. Draw a row of ten palm trees similar to the cocoanut palm, Fig. 14, extending away and to the right.

14. Draw palm trees similar to Fig. 13 in place of the trees of Fig. 18.

15. Combine all of the palm trees in the place of the trees of Fig. 18.

16. Figs. 19-25 are trees that have been drawn as they appeared silhouetted against the sky. Take the class out of doors and find trees similar to these, with the sky as a background, and let the pupils draw them in mass as they appear to the eye.

17. Place a plant in such a position as to make it practically of one shade and let the pupils draw it.

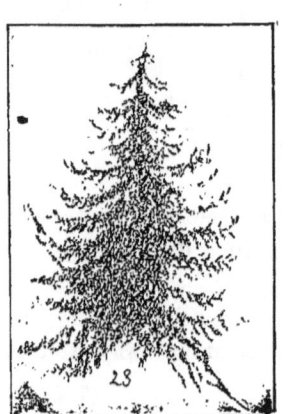

18. Procure sprays of leaves or vines and draw them as in Fig. 17.

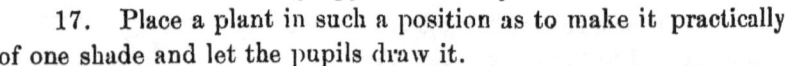

Automatic Processes. — In arithmetic there are and should be certain processes that are purely automatic, such as the processes of addition and the multiplication table. In language the words of ordinary conversation are spoken automatically, in obedience to the thought which they express. Writing is and should be purely automatic so that the

whole attention may be given to the thought expressed by the written characters. In like manner there are certain processes in drawing that should become largely automatic, before rapid progress can be made in the art. Among these processes may be mentioned *the perspective principle, proportion, and the manipulation of the pencil.*

The **Perspective Principle** consists of representing objects on a flat surface at seemingly different distances away, as they appear in nature.

The elements of this principle may be taught to pupils of the second grade or even lower. Below are simple methods of inculcating this principle.

1. Draw on the blackboard a line similar to AB, Fig. 26. Draw an object, say a post, at each end of the line, as posts 1 and 2. Post 2 may be any size smaller than post 1.

2. Ask the pupils to draw another post half way between posts 1 and 2. Post 3, Fig. 27. Do not draw this post in your drawing, but let the pupils draw it according to their judgment. You may, however, lead them to see that this post will be smaller than post 1, and larger than post 2.

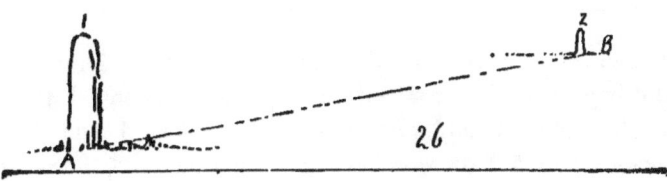

3. In like manner ask them to draw post 4 half-way between posts 1 and 3, and post 5, half-way between posts 3 and 2.

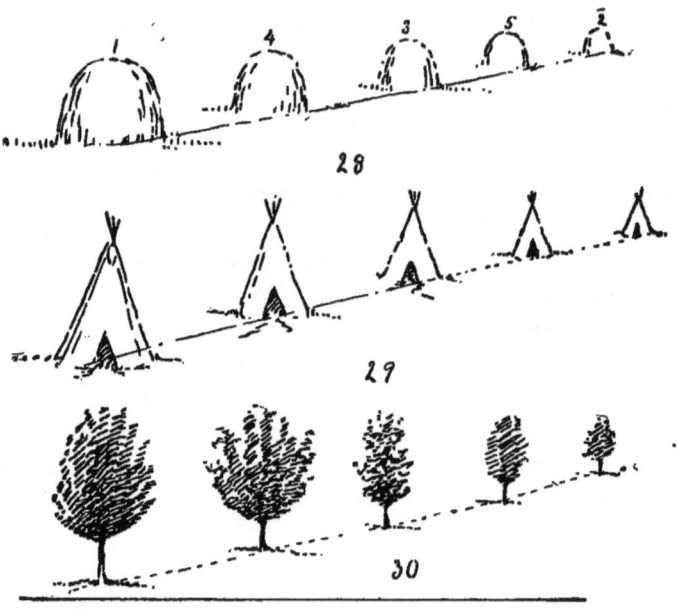

In the same manner use hay-cocks, Fig. 28. Draw the light line and hay-cocks 1 and 2 with the pupils. Then ask the pupils to draw hay-cock 3 half-way between hay-cocks 1 and 2. Then hay-cocks 4 and 5 half-way between 1 and 3, and 3 and 2. In like manner draw the wigwams and trees, Figs. 29 and 30.

AUGSBURG'S DRAWING. 67

Draw a row of posts on line AB, Fig. 31, in the same manner as in Fig. 27.

Draw a line parallel with line AB, similar to line CD, and dictate to the class as follows:

Draw at the right of post 1, on line CD, a ball. Draw at the right of post 3, on line CD, a ball. Do the same at the right of post 2. Post 4. Post 5.

Draw another line, as EF, and go through the same drill as above, using a rock, or other object, in the same manner as the ball.

Two or more objects of different size may be associated together, as the wigwams and trees in Fig. 32.

Draw the row of trees the same as the posts, Fig. 27. Lead the pupils to see that a wigwam is smaller than a tree, then let them draw a row of trees in the same manner as the posts, Fig. 27.

Then dictate: At the right of tree 1 draw a wigwam. Draw a wigwam at the right of tree 4. At the right of tree 3; tree 5; tree 2. The wigwams may be placed at the right, left, in front, or back of each tree.

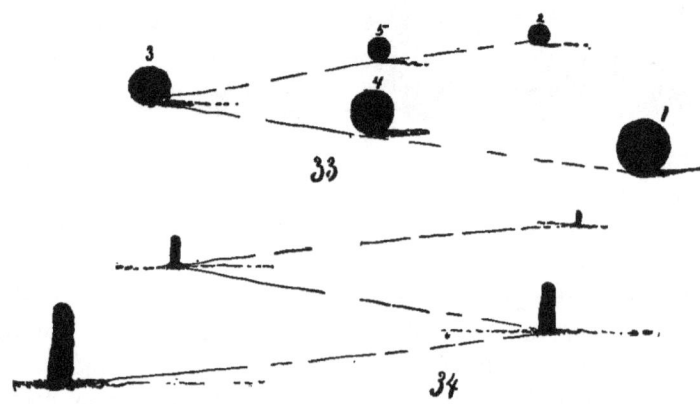

The objects may be arranged as the balls in Fig. 33, or as the posts in Fig. 34.

Draw the line 1, 3, 2, and the balls 1 and 2. Dictate as follows:

Draw a ball at angle 3. Draw a ball half-way between balls 1 and 3.

AUGSBURG'S DRAWING. 69

Draw a ball half-way between balls 3 and 2.
Draw a ball at the left of ball 1. At the right of ball 3. In front of ball 4. Back of ball 5, etc.
Substitute hay-cocks, trees, wigwams, or similar objects, in the place of the balls and posts of Figs. 33 and 34.
Draw on the blackboard a base-ball diamond, similar to Fig. 35. Draw the boy striking, and the one on second base, and then let the pupils draw the boys on the first and third bases, the short stop, catcher, pitcher, right, left, and center-fielders, umpire, etc.
By combining these figures and objects an endless variety of exercises may be given, until the perspective principle has, at least in part, become automatic.

36

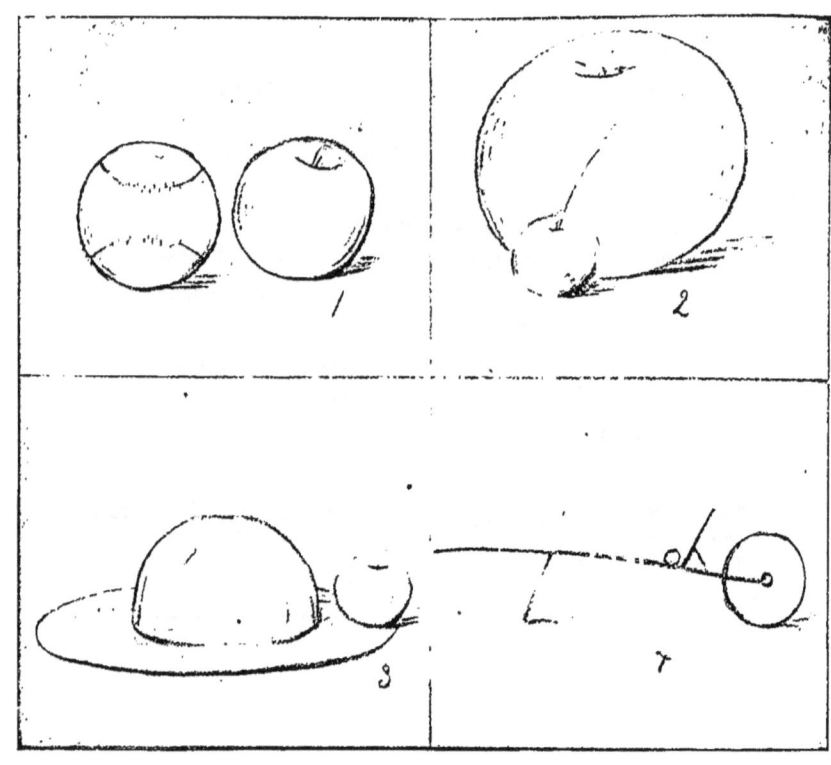

CHAPTER VI.

Relative Size of Objects.

To represent the relative size or proportion of objects is perhaps the most essential mechanical element in good drawing. This relative size is difficult for pupils to see and represent without aid from the teacher. The following is a simple and quite effective method of teaching this, while leading the pupil to note the relative difference in the size of objects.

It is necessary to choose some object for a unit of measure or comparison, that all children are acquainted with, such as a ball or apple. In this chapter we will use an apple.

Place on the blackboard a ball, a cherry, a hat, and a wheelbarrow. Figs. 1, 2, 3, and 4.

Ask the class to show with their thumbs and forefingers about how large a ball is, then how large an apple is. Draw from them

the fact that they are about the same size. If possible hold up an apple and ball together, that the pupils may see that they are about the same size.

Draw the apple on the blackboard by the side of the ball, as in Fig. 1.

Ask the class to show with their curved forefingers and thumbs

AUGSBURG'S DRAWING. 73

how large a cherry is, then how large an apple is. Draw from them the fact that a cherry is much smaller than an apple.

If possible show an apple and cherry to the class.

Draw the apple by the cherry, as in Fig. 2.

In like manner compare the hat and apple. The wheelbarrow and apple. Figs. 3 and 4.

Place an acorn, Fig. 8, on the blackboard and ask a pupil to draw an apple by the side of it. Let the other pupils judge whether the proportion is correct. In like manner place a walnut, Fig. 7; a berry basket, Fig. 6; a hay-cock and a tree, Fig. 5; and ask pupils to draw an apple by the side of each.

Use the real objects whenever possible to aid the comparison.

Draw on the blackboard a hay-cock, tree, berry-basket, walnut, and acorn, and ask the pupils to copy them on their tablets, and to place an apple by the side of each.

Place on the blackboard various objects, such as Figs. 9–16, and let the pupils copy them, both on the blackboard and on their tablets, and by each place an apple of the right size and proportion. Until they have tried and failed, do not aid the pupils in making this comparison.

It is an excellent plan to represent the size of the apple by means of height and width lines.

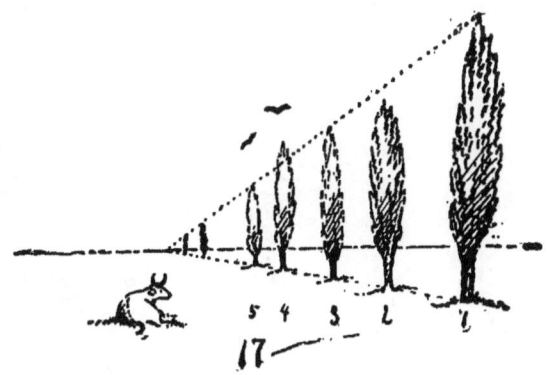

74   AUGSBURG'S DRAWING.

Any object the pupils are familiar with may be used as a unit of comparison, such as a base-ball, foot-ball, pear, or pumpkin. The object used should be easy to represent. Always use models whenever possible; the progress is more rapid and the results more sure when this is done.

Draw on the blackboard a row of trees.

Represent trees 1, 3, and 5 of the same height, and tree 2 shorter and tree 4 taller than the others.

Ask a pupil to point to the nearest tree.

The tree farthest away.

The shortest tree.

The tallest tree.

The trees of the same height.

Lead the pupils to see that the further away the object, the smaller it is drawn.

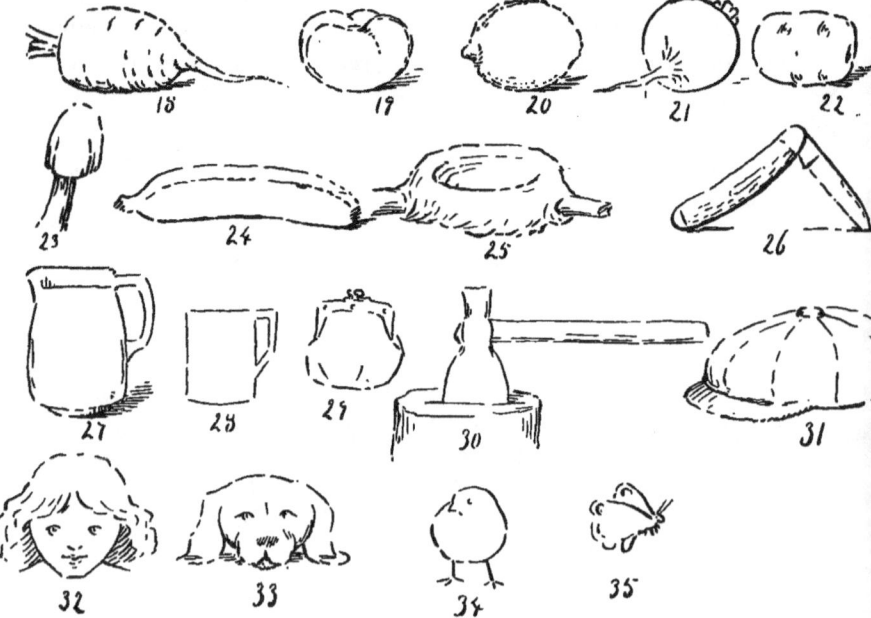

DRILL EXERCISES

1. Draw a carrot and an apple.
2. Draw a tomato and an apple.
3. Draw a lemon and an apple.
4. Draw a turnip and an apple.
5. Draw a potato and an apple.
6. Draw a toadstool and an apple.
7. Draw a banana and an apple.
8. Draw a bird's nest and an apple.
9. Draw a pocket-knife and an apple.
10. Draw a pitcher and an apple.
11. Draw a mug and an apple.
12. Draw a wallet and an apple.
13. Draw a hatchet and an apple.
14. Draw a cap and an apple.
15. Place an apple on the head of Fig. 32.
16. Place an apple by the side of the dog's head,
17. Place an apple behind the chick, Fig. 34.
18. Draw a hat and place an apple in it.
19. Place the spider, Fig. 9, on an apple.
20. Draw a peanut and an apple.
21. Draw a foot-ball and an apple.
22. Draw a walnut and an apple.
23. Draw an acorn and an apple.
24. Draw a squash and an apple.
25. Draw a frog and an apple.
26. Draw a cat and an apple.
27. Draw a rabbit and an apple.
28. Draw a squirrel and an apple.
29. Draw a mouse and an apple.
30. Draw a bird and an apple.

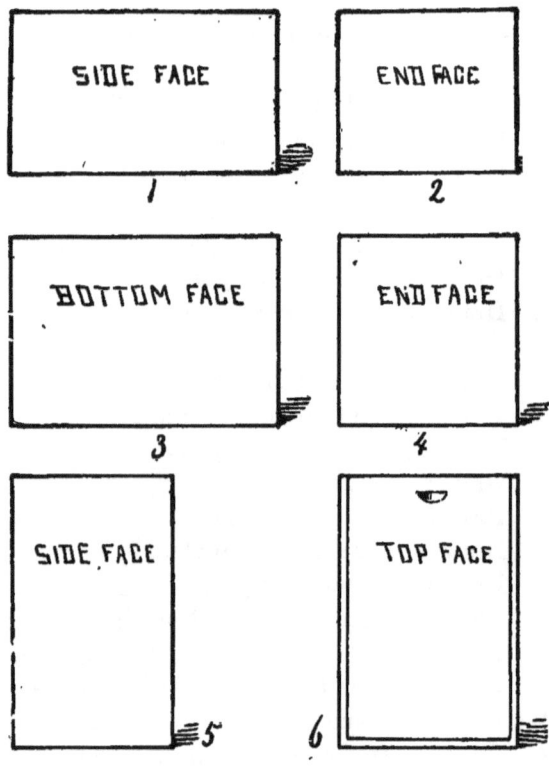

CHAPTER VII.

Teaching Proportion.

Models.—A common crayon box is one of the best models to teach the recognition of the proportion of square-cornered forms. It has no superior in the variety of its faces and in its convenience and adaptability as a model.

If preferred, faces made of cardboard may be used. There should be four of each kind, cut 7 x 7, 7 x 8, 7 x 9, 7 x 10, 7 x 11 and 7 x 12 inches. The cardboard models are to be used the same as the crayon box faces.

The following are good methods for teaching proportion:

1. Hold the side of the crayon box towards the class and ask each pupil to find a similar shape in the room. Call on a pupil for his form, and then let the class decide whether it is similar to the shape of the side of the box or not. *It is the proportion and not the size, that pupils are to recognize.* Turn the box with the end view to the class and ask them, as before, to find a similar shape. Do not take up a whole recitation in this kind of work, but spend a few moments at the beginning of each recitation, until pupils can recognize proportion readily. There are always plenty of objects in the school-room that have faces similar to each face of the box, such as door, panel, transom, window, glass, blackboard, wall, ceiling, floor, chart, card, map, picture, book, top of table, desk, platform, etc.

2. Draw all the faces of the box, Figs. 1–6, on the black-board. Ask the class how face 1 differs from face 5; face 2 from face 4; face 3 from face 6.

In connection with these exercises teach the following words: vertical, horizontal, parallel, right angle, square and rectangle. The word *rectangle* is better than the word *oblong* as applied to Figs. 1–6.

Figs. 1, 2 and 3 may be called *horizontal rectangles*, and Figs. 4, 5 and 6, *vertical rectangles*. Teach the above words with *the model*, with *the drawing* and with *similar forms* in the room.

(NOTE.— Some teachers have trouble to draw the faces on the blackboard in the right proportion. This is overcome by cutting out the different faces from pasteboard double the size of the crayon box face, then marking the corners with a lead pencil on the blackboard. Do this before the class is called, and then draw the faces on the blackboard while the class is present.)

3. Draw faces 1–6 on the blackboard. Hold a face of the box toward the class and ask them to find on the blackboard the rectangle that represents it. Do so with all the faces.

78   AUGSBURG'S DRAWING.

4. Draw face 1 on the blackboard. Give the box to a pupil and ask him to find on the box the face represented on the blackboard. Teach the pupil to hold the box at arms' length and on a level with his eye when looking for the face. In like manner drill with all the faces. Teach him to compare intelligently.

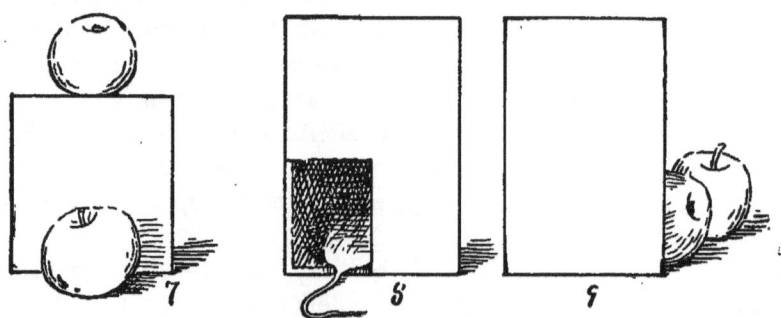

5. Place several boxes in position (one in front of each alternate aisle is perhaps the best place) where the pupils can plainly see the face, say face 1. Let each pupil draw this face on his tablet. Pass among the pupils and kindly criticise those who have not drawn the form correctly, by holding the face of the box before them, and asking them to compare their drawing with it. *This is the lesson proper.*

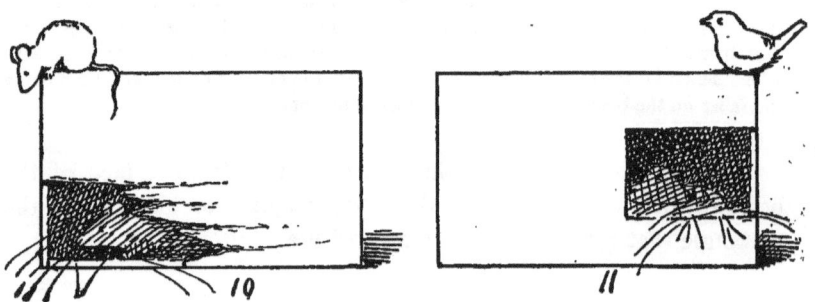

AUGSBURG'S DRAWING. 79

Draw this face again on the blackboard and turn it into some other object shaped like the face, and let the pupils do the same.

The drawings in this chapter are in form similar to the sides of the crayon box. The aims in these drawings are:

1. As a device to make the forms interesting.
2. To show the similiarity between the faces of the box and similarly formed objects both large and small.
3. To teach picture making. In turning these faces into various other objects the different kinds of line, methods of expression, and technique that are so difficult to teach with the real object, may be readily taught through imitation.

Do not turn the rectangle into another form, or add devices until the lesson in proportion is complete. For example, do not place the form, Fig. 7, on the blackboard or add the apples until all pupils have reproduced the face of the box on their tablets in the right proportion.

The houses represented in Figs. 14–18 are alike in form but differ in the *arrangement of details and the materials of which they are composed.* They are all drawn as follows:

1. Draw the rectangle ABCD, Fig. 14. 2. Bisect AB as

at E and from this point draw the vertical line as high as the apex F is to be, and draw lines FA and FB.

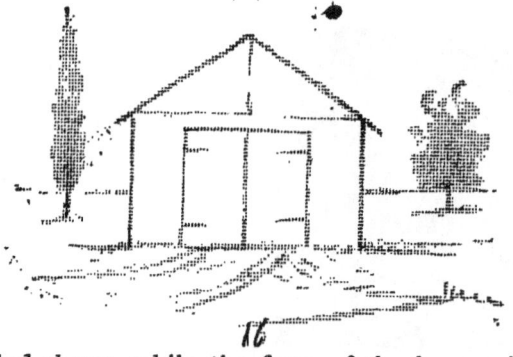

As stated above, while the form of the houses is the same, they differ in the arrangement of the details and in the representa-

tion of the materials of which they are composed. Fig. 15 is to represent a hen house built of boards; Fig. 16, a barn. Fig. 17 represents a stone house; and Fig. 18, a log house.

All of these houses may be introduced in connection with the forms of Figs. 1-6.

Figs. 19-22 represent the same landscape adapted to various shaped rectangles. Place any simple landscape on the blackboard, and then adapt to various shaped rectangles.

Figs. 23-25 represent the three principal triangles. Cut four of each triangle from paste-board or similar material. Cut each base 9 inches long, and teach the pupils to draw them on their tablets the same as they did the rectangles, Figs. 1-6.

82   AUGSBURG'S DRAWING.

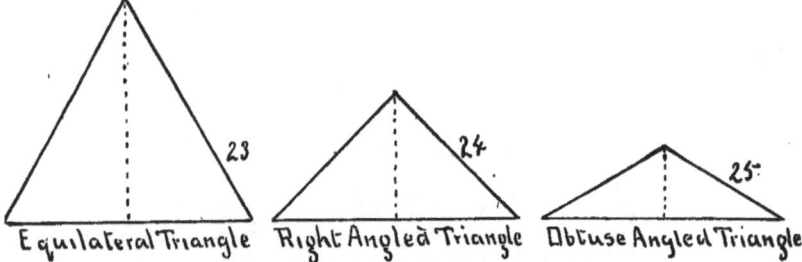

Teach the words — *triangle, equilateral, right-angle, obtuse-angle, altitude,* and *oblique.*

The roofs of Figs. 14–18 are all obtuse-angled triangles. These may be drawn first, and the rectangle representing the body of the house added to the triangle if so desired.

The roofs of Figs. 31 and 39 are both equilateral triangles. The roofs of Figs. 33 and 38 are right-angled triangles,

and the roofs of 29, 34, 35, and 36 are right-angled triangles. See Figs. 24 or 25.

A semi-circular form may be taught in the same manner, and be made the basis of Figs. 32, 37, and 50.

Chalk Drawing.— Children enjoy quickness in drawing. They love to represent an idea at every stroke if possible, and to repeat this idea over and over. For these reasons drawings similar to Figs. 26-50 are especially pleasing to them. In putting such designs on the blackboard the *side of short pieces of crayon is used*. If a lead pencil is used, it should be sharpened flat like a chisel — chisel-shaped — but the best result is with a short piece of crayon on the blackboard.

The advantages of such drawing are as follows :
1. By using the side of the crayon the lines are more firm.
2. An idea is represented with each stroke of the pencil, and is repeated an indefinite number of times, thus giving much practice.

3. There are few obstructions and no erasing. For example, in Fig. 43, the posts are drawn directly through the fence boards.

4. The lines are not suggestive, but positive and direct, a feature that is peculiarly attractive to children.

Figs. 26–50 being based on the rectangular and triangular forms, are drawn in the same manner as Figs. 10–22.

DRILL EXERCISES.

1. Find in the room a similar form to Fig. 1.
2. Find in the room a similar form to Fig. 5.
3. Find in the room a similar form to Fig. 2
4. Find in the room a similar form to Fig. 4.
5. Find in the room a similar form to Fig. 3.
6. Find in the room a similar form to Fig. 6.

Draw on the blackboard faces 1, 2, 3, 4, 5 and 6 double the size of the original crayon box, and drill as follows:

7. How does face 1 differ from face 5?
8. How does face 2 differ from face 4?
9. Point to a vertical line in the drawing. To two vertical lines. Find a vertical line on the box. Two vertical lines. Hold your arm in a vertical position. Find a vertical line in the room. Two. Three.
10. Point to a horizontal line in the drawing. To two horizontal lines. To six horizontal lines. Find a horizontal line on your desk. In the room.
11. Point to two vertical parallel lines. Find two vertical parallel lines on the box. Find three. Four. Hold your arms in a parallel horizontal position. Find two parallel horizontal lines on your desk. In the room. Find three. Four.
12. Find a right-angle in the drawing. Find two. Three. Four. Find one on your desk. In the room.
13. Draw on your tablet or the blackboard a vertical line.

A horizontal line. A right-angle. Two vertical parallel lines. Two horizontal parallel lines.

14. Give a crayon box to a pupil and ask him to find on it Face 1. Face 5. Face 3. Face 6. Face 2. Face 4, as you point to them on the blackboard.

15. Point to Face 1 on the box and ask a pupil to find it on the blackboard. Face 2. Face 3. Face 4. Face 5. Face 6.

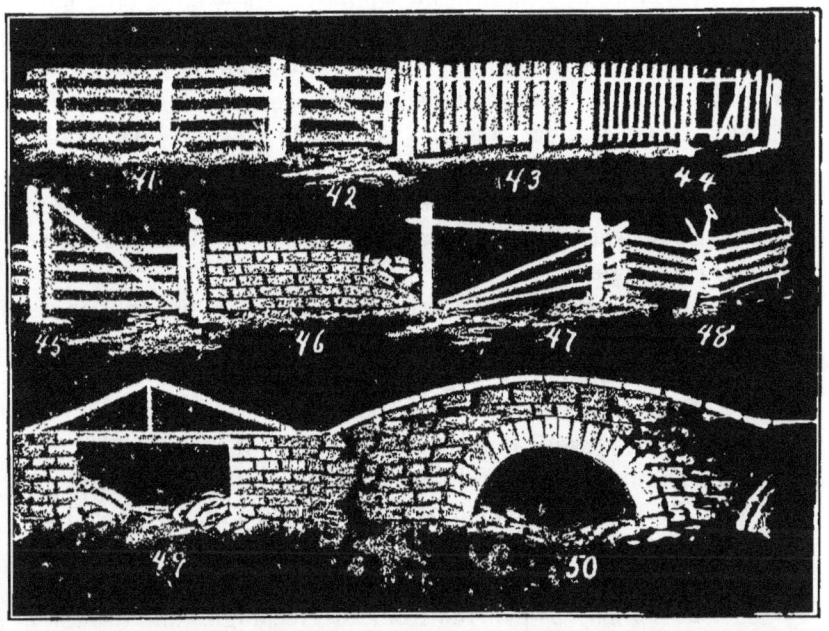

16. Have the pupils draw Face 1 of the box. Turn it into a cage, Fig. 12.

17. Have the pupils draw Face 2 of the box. Turn it into Fig. 10, or Fig. 11.

18. Have the pupils draw Face 3 of the box Turn it into Fig. 13.

19. Have the pupils draw Face 1 of the box, and turn it into Fig. 16. Fig. 17. Fig. 18.

20. Draw on the blackboard Fig. 19. Have the pupils draw on their tablets Face 1, and place the landscape in it.

21. Draw Fig. 22 and have it placed in Face 5.

22. Draw Fig. 21 and place it in Face 4.

Place the triangles along the blackboard rail.

23. Charles may choose an equilateral triangle. A right-angled triangle; an obtuse-angled triangle.

How does the equilateral triangle differ from the right-angled triangle? From the obtuse-angled triangle?

24. Draw a right angle. An acute angle. An obtuse angle.

25. Draw an equilateral triangle. Show what equilateral means. Show what altitude means. What kind of angles has an equilateral triangle?

26. Draw a right-angled triangle. Point to the right angle. What are the other two angles?

27. Draw an obtuse-angled triangle. Point to the obtuse angle. What are the other two angles?

28. Draw an equilateral triangle. Turn it into Fig. 28.

29. Draw an equilateral triangle. Turn it into Fig. 30.

30. Draw a right-angled triangle. Add Fig. 1 to it. Turn it into Fig. 33.

In like manner all the various houses and fences represented by Figs. 26–50 may be evolved from the rectangles and triangles, Figs. 1–6 and 23–25.

CHAPTER VIII.

Teaching Unity.

Relative Size, Proportion and Unity of Form are different names for very much the same concept.

The relative size may be called the relation of objects and parts of objects to themselves; as the relative size of the eyes, nose, mouth and head; or the bowl, handle, lid and nose of a teapot.

Proportion may be called the relation of geometrical forms to themselves and similar forms, as the proportion of rectangles; the proportion of a rectangle to the side of a barn. *Unity* may be called the relation of geometrical form to dissimilar objects, as the relation of a triangle to a tree top or a sail boat.

Unity in Drawing is the ability to see and recognize objects or a collection of objects as a whole — as a unit; to see and unite the parts of an object or several objects in right relationship.

Children naturally see objects as a whole, but the moment they attempt to reproduce them in drawing, the *oneness* is largely lost and each part, to them, becomes a unit by itself. Ask a child to draw a bird, and he will begin with some smaller part, such as the bill, and draw each part with but little relation to the whole bird. The power of seeing and reproducing an object as a whole must be acquired—must be taught to children.

Method of Teaching Unity. —An excellent method of teaching unity to children is to teach the triangle, square, rectangle or oblong, circle, oval and ellipse (Figs. 12–19), and then apply the knowledge in the drawing of objects. There are few forms, however complicated they may be, that cannot wholly or in part be proportioned by these forms. Figs 12–19 may be taught by cutting the figures from cardboard, and then teaching their form as shown in this chapter.

It is not enough to simply know the names of these forms, and to be able to recognize their shape; they must be understood to the extent that they can be used—used as a *measure of form*, as type forms. It can be truly said that a pupil does not know these forms until he can draw them. The test of his knowledge is his ability to use the forms in connection with his work.

Teaching Geometrical Forms.— Cut from cardboard or similar material the following geometrical forms: Three right-angled and three obtuse-angled triangles with the longest side 4, 7 and 9 inches long. Figs. 13 and 14.

Three equilateral triangles 4, 7 and 9 inches long on each side. Fig. 12.
Three squares, 3, 6 and 8 inches square. Fig. 15.
Three rectangles or oblongs, 5 x 6, 5 x 7 and 5 x 8 inches. Fig. 16.

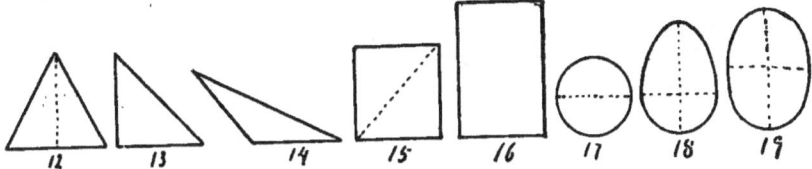

Three circles, 3, 6 and 8 inches in diameter. Fig. 17.
Three ovals and three ellipses, 3, 6 and 8 inches long.

Teach these forms in three groups: (1) The triangles, (2) the square and rectangle, (3) the circle, oval and ellipse.

Teach each form: (1) on the model, (2) in the drawing, (3) its application.

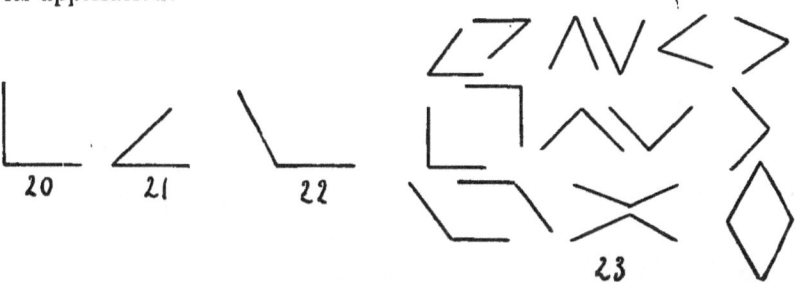

Draw on the blackboard the three angles — right, acute and obtuse.

Lead the pupils to see what a right angle is. Do not describe it, let them see it.

Example—George, point to a right angle on this book. To another. To another. Still another. Show me a right angle with your fingers. Find a right angle in this room.

All may look for a moment, and then at a signal, point to a right angle in the room. To another. Another.

Lead the pupils to see that an acute angle is less, and an obtuse angle is more than a right angle.

All may stand. With your forefingers make a right angle. Acute angle. Obtuse angle. With your arms make a right angle. An acute angle. An obtuse angle. With your forefinger mark in the air a right angle. An acute angle. An obtuse angle.

Draw on your tablets a right angle. An acute angle. An obtuse angle.

Draw on the blackboard right, acute and obtuse angles as in Fig. 23.

Helen may take the pointer and find three acute angles, three right angles, three obtuse angles.

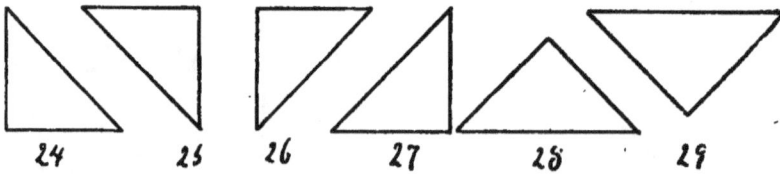

Draw on the blackboard a right-angled triangle. Fig. 24.

Tell the pupils the meaning of " tri " and that triangle means a figure with three angles.

John, point to a right angle in the triangle. Can you find more than one right angle? What are the other two angles?

Draw Figs. 24–29 on the blackboard. Julia, point to a right angle in each. What are the other two angles in each?

Robert, take this card board triangle and hold it in the position of Fig. 24, Fig. 25, Fig. 26, Fig. 27, Fig. 28, Fig. 29.

All may stand. Hold the right-angled triangle in the position of Fig. 24 and ask the pupils to draw it in the air with their fingers. Change it to Fig. 25 and let them do the same. Fig. 26, Fig. 27, Fig. 28, Fig. 29.

In the same manner let the pupils draw the right angled triangle on their tablets.

In like manner, teach all the geometrical forms, Figs. 12-19.

The reasons for teaching these forms are:

They are standard forms.

Children can learn and understand these forms at a very early age.

They will aid the pupil to see and grasp the form and proportion of other forms, both similar and dissimilar.

Recognizing these forms in other objects makes the reproduction of those objects more simple and easy.

They are a great aid in remembering the form and proportion of objects.

Applying the Form Knowledge.—The following methods are to show how to apply this knowledge to the study of objects both real and in pictures, to the end that complicated objects may be made more simple and their form more easily grasped.

Procure a round, an oval and an elliptical shaped apple or similar objects, Figs. 32, 33 and 34. Place these apples before the class and ask pupils to pick out the round apple; the oblong or elliptical apple; the oval apple.

Draw these apples on the blackboard and ask the pupils to point to each form. Point to a drawing and ask a pupil to point to the apple it represents. Point to an apple and ask a pupil to point to the drawing it represents.

Draw on the blackboard a circle, oval, ellipse and square and turn each into a padlock.

Mary, take the pointer and point to a round padlock. A square one. A triangular shaped one. An oval one. An elliptical one.

George, trace the circle in one of the padlocks; the ellipse; the oval; the square; the triangle.

All may draw a square; a circle; an oval and an ellipse on their tablets. Turn each into a padlock.

In like manner use the teapot, Figs. 9–12.

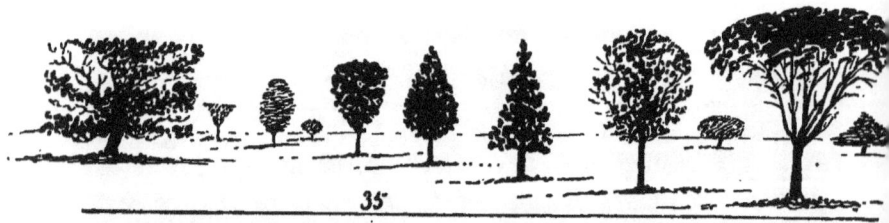

Draw on the blackboard trees similar to Fig. 35 and let a pupil point to a tree with a round top, with an elliptical top, a triangular top, a rectangular top and an oval top.

Ask the pupils to draw on their tablets a tree with an oval top, a triangular top, a rectangular top.

Lead the pupils to observe these forms in tree tops. One who has never observed the shape of tree tops will be surprised to find how often geometrical forms occur in such seemingly complicated forms.

Fig. 47 represents a landscape, in which the trees, mountain, lake, hills and road are all triangular, showing to what an extent a landscape may be made up of these forms.

A knowledge of these forms is a great aid in the drawing of animals, where quickness of observation and speed in execution are desirable.

In Fig 30 observe that the shape of the body is rectangular, and that of the pig, in Fig. 31, is elliptical. The bodies of the rabbits, Figs. 36 and 39, are oval, and in Figs. 37 and 38 are elliptical. To recognize these shapes is a great aid in "blocking-in" the general form of animals.

Even in as complicated an object as the human head, these forms can be readily traced, and when once recognized, greatly aid in making the general proportions.

Head 40 is square. Heads 41 and 42 are oval. Heads 43 and 44 are square. Head 45 is triangular. The hair and faces in heads 40, 43 and 44 are triangular.

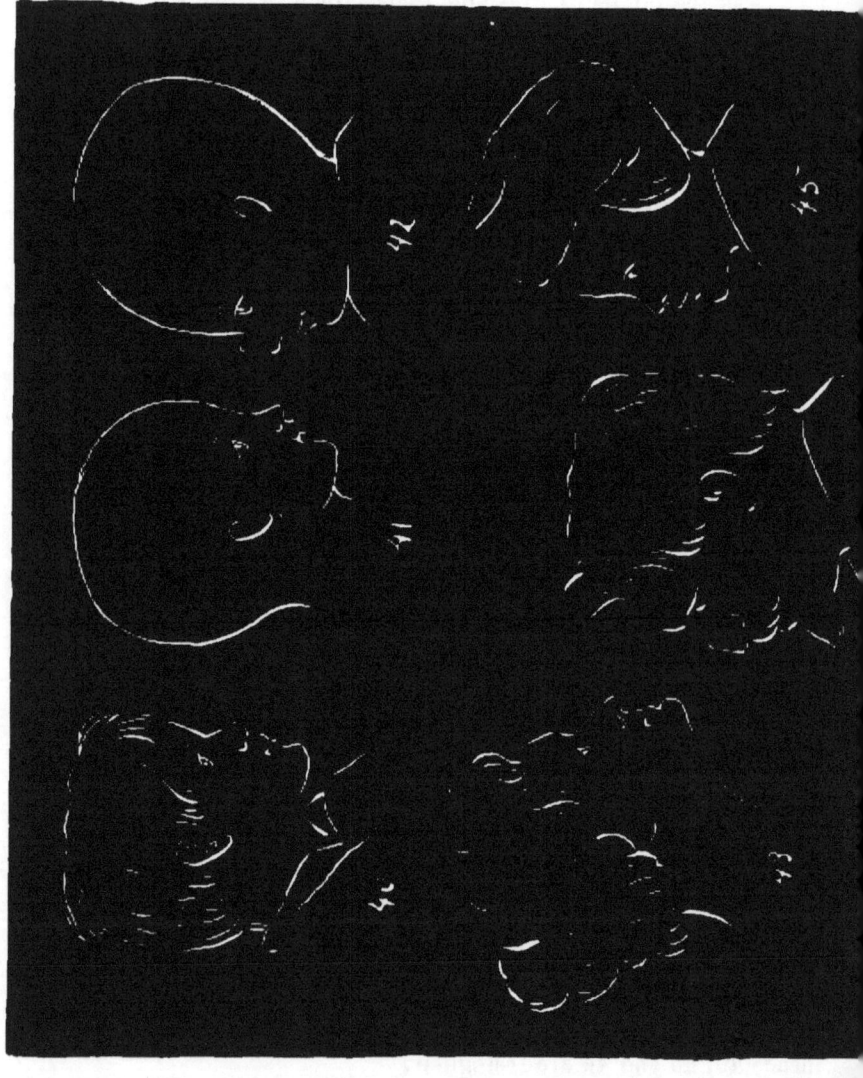

Fig. 46 is made up almost entirely of squares. Head, waist, dress and legs, are each contained in squares.

DRILL EXERCISES.

1. Form with your forefingers a right angle. An acute angle. An obtuse angle. Form with your arms a right angle. Acute angle. Obtuse angle.

2. Draw on the blackboard a right angle. An acute angle. An obtuse angle.

3. Find in the room a right angle. An acute angle. An obtuse angle.

(NOTE.— Tell the pupils that the right angle is made almost exclusively by man and is seldom seen in nature. The acute and the obtuse angles are the predominating lines found in nature. Ask the pupils to try and find a right angle in nature that has not been made by the hand of man.)

4. Draw a right angle. Acute angle. Obtuse angle. Write the name of each angle.

5. Hold up the cardboard triangle in the position of Fig. 24 and let the pupils draw it; Fig. 25, Fig. 26, Fig. 27, Fig. 28, Fig. 29.

6. Draw an equilateral triangle. What does equilateral mean?

7. Hold the cardboard equilateral triangle in the position of Fig. 28 and let the class draw it. In the position of Fig. 29.

8. Draw a right, equilateral and obtuse-angled triangle, all in the position of Fig. 28. In the position of Fig. 29.

9. What angles has a right-angled triangle? An equilateral triangle? An obtuse-angled triangle?

10. Draw a square on the blackboard. What kind of angles has it? How many angles has it? How many sides has it? Which side is the longest?

11. Draw a square. Draw a square shaped like a diamond.

12. Draw a square. Draw a diagonal. Into what does the diagonal divide the square?

13. Draw a rectangle on the blackboard. How does it differ from a square?

(NOTE.—Fig. 16 is often called an oblong, but this is a general term meaning longer one way than the other. Rectangle also includes the square, but we seldom speak of the square as a rectangle, thus leaving the word rectangle as applying to a square-cornered figure longer one way than the other.

The term *vertical rectangle* means a rectangle longer vertically than horizontally. A *horizontal rectangle* is one longer horizontally than vertically.)

14. Draw a vertical rectangle. A horizontal rectangle.

15. Draw a short vertical rectangle. A long vertical rectangle. A short horizontal rectangle. A long horizontal rectangle.

16. Draw a circle, an oval and an ellipse on the blackboard. How does the oval differ from the ellipse? What is the oval shaped like? Are both ends of the oval alike? Are both ends of the ellipse alike?

17. Draw a circle. An oval. An ellipse.

18. Draw a wide oval. A narrow oval.

19. Draw a wide ellipse. A narrow ellipse.

20. Draw an oval with the smaller end pointing downward. Upward. To the right. To the left.

21. Draw a vertical ellipse. Draw a horizontal ellipse. Draw an oblique ellipse.

22. Place Figs. 12–19 on the blackboard. Helen, take this pointer and point to a circle. An equilateral triangle. A right-angled triangle. An obtuse-angled triangle. A square. A rectangle. An oval. An ellipse. A right angle. Obtuse angle. Acute angle. A diameter. A diagonal.

23. Class may draw in the air: A right angle. Obtuse angle. Acute angle. Square. A vertical rectangle. A horizontal rectangle. A circle. An ellipse. An oval. An equilateral triangle. A right-angled triangle. An obtuse-angled triangle.

24. What is the shape of this book? The window? The transom? This blackboard? The top of this cap? The opening of the door? etc.

25. Find an object shaped like a circle. Square. Rectangle. Oval. Ellipse. Triangle.

26. Draw a round apple. An oval apple. An elliptical apple.

27. Draw a round padlock. A square padlock. An oval padlock. An elliptical padlock.

28. Draw a round, oval, elliptical, rectangular and triangular teapot.

29. Draw a tree with an oval top. An elliptical top. A triangular top.

CHAPTER IX.

Primary Object Drawing.

The Model.— The use of the model in drawing is *to form, and correct,* the image in the child's mind. If the child has never seen the object, then a new image is formed. If the child has seen the object, or if an image has already been formed, then it is the function of the model to correct and make more perfect this image. *It is this image, and not the model, that the child reproduces in drawing.* The model before the child invites him to look again, to compare, to perfect, to make the image in the mind like the model.

The Copy or Drawing.— The office of the drawing or copy is to show *how to represent the image that the mind has formed.* There is nothing in the object or model to show how to represent it on a flat surface. The drawing does this. The model *represents the idea,* the drawing *how to represent the idea on a flat surface.* The model is *the source,* the drawing is *the how* and represents the technique, or the mode of expression.

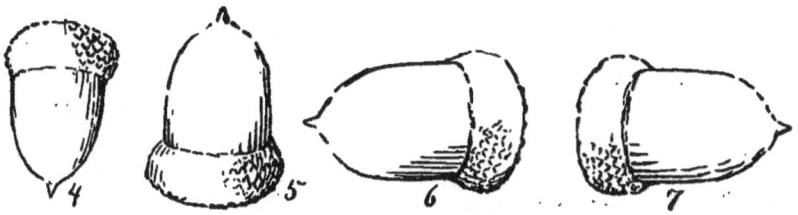

Teaching Drawing.— The most effective means of teaching drawing to children is by example. The teacher must lead, not push, must *draw*, not talk, must show how by drawing, not by explaining. What has been your great desire when you wanted to make this or that and did not know how?— Oh, if I could only see some one do it! If I could only *see*. If this is true with you, how much more is it with little children, who are all eyes, and who see, imitate, and do, in the superlative degree?

How does a boy learn how to swim? (1) He sees other boys swim. (2) He wants to swim. (3) Given the opportunity, he learns. It is the same with flying kites, jumping the rope, riding a bicycle, etc. They *see*, they have the *desire*, they *learn*. Your pupils will learn drawing in precisely the same way if they have the opportunity.

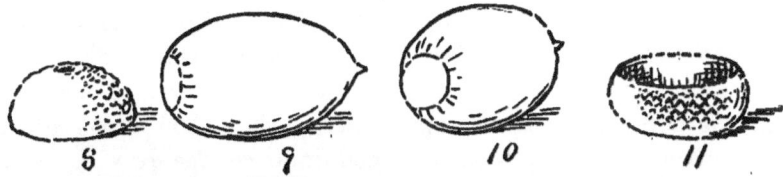

A Method of Teaching.— Ask *one* of your pupils (not the whole school) to procure for you as many acorns as you have pupils (leaves, buds, flowers, fruit, nuts, shells, etc., of various kinds will do as well).

First Step.— Give an acorn to each pupil and let them begin to draw an outline picture of it at once. Teach them to hold the acorn in the left hand and draw with the right. Teach them to look carefully at the acorn first and then begin to draw, then to look again and do the same. The TRY is what you are after, not the *drawing*.

The reasons for holding small objects in one hand and drawing them with the other, are:

    1. Convenience, especially when drawing at the blackboard.

    2. The object is naturally held in a good and easy position and may be studied to the best advantage.

    3. The method is always available and each pupil can attend to his own model without the teacher's aid.

Second Step.—Step to the blackboard with an acorn between your thumb and forefinger and draw a picture of it on the blackboard, similar to Fig. 3. The pupils have probably made their drawing similar to Fig. 1, without the least expression and with one unalterable line. This is right, but we must extend the range of the line. Now, if you afterwards place your drawing on the board they will have something for comparison. They will see that you *first sketch your acorn with light lines*, as in Fig. 2, carefully blocking in the proportion and then finish it with heavier and accented lines, as in Fig. 3. Don't talk, don't explain, don't say a word; simply draw, and bright eyes will do the rest. Your drawing is not for them to copy, but to show how, to lead, to encourage. The pupils see how you draw, see the drawing on the blackboard and try to do likewise. To be sure there will be more or less copying of your drawing, but never mind, this is a tendency inborn in the human race and is a force that will serve you well if rightly directed; so when looking at the drawings of each do not judge harshly those who have copied your drawing, but lead them to draw what they see; to draw their own acorn.

Turn the acorn over and draw it with the point upward, as in Fig. 5. There is no reason why pupils should not draw from two to six acorns in one lesson, and draw each as well as if only one was drawn. Slow, laborious drawing, in a class of little ones, is not desirable or profitable. Drawing is not slow work unless it is made so. Children are full of life, action and vigor; they love quickness as well in the drawing-class as in their sports, so do not allow the class to lag, but draw the acorn in many positions — with the point down, up, to the right, to the left. Draw the acorn with the cap removed. Draw the cap in various positions. Figs. 4-12 represent the various positions that may be drawn.

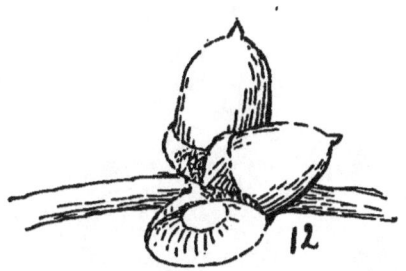

Cut some twigs containing bunches of acorns, similar to Fig. 12, and let the pupils draw them.

A good way to save time is to place small objects on the chalk rail of the blackboard, where they may be available for instant use, both at the blackboard and seats.

Children's Interest in Form.—Of all the attributes of objects and things, children are the least interested in form. They are interested in the *life* and *action*, the *color*, and the *use* of things, but about the form, for form's sake, they care little. They love animals and birds because they are alive; they love flowers for their color; they love guns, marbles, kites. etc.. for their use;

they love dolls because they suggest life; but they seldom love an object for its beauty of form.

Devices.—After the children have drawn the acorns in several positions, and have become a little weary, interest may be revived and carried through almost any number of lessons by a judicious use of devices. As children are so passionately fond of life, connect life with the object they are drawing. Figs. 13–18

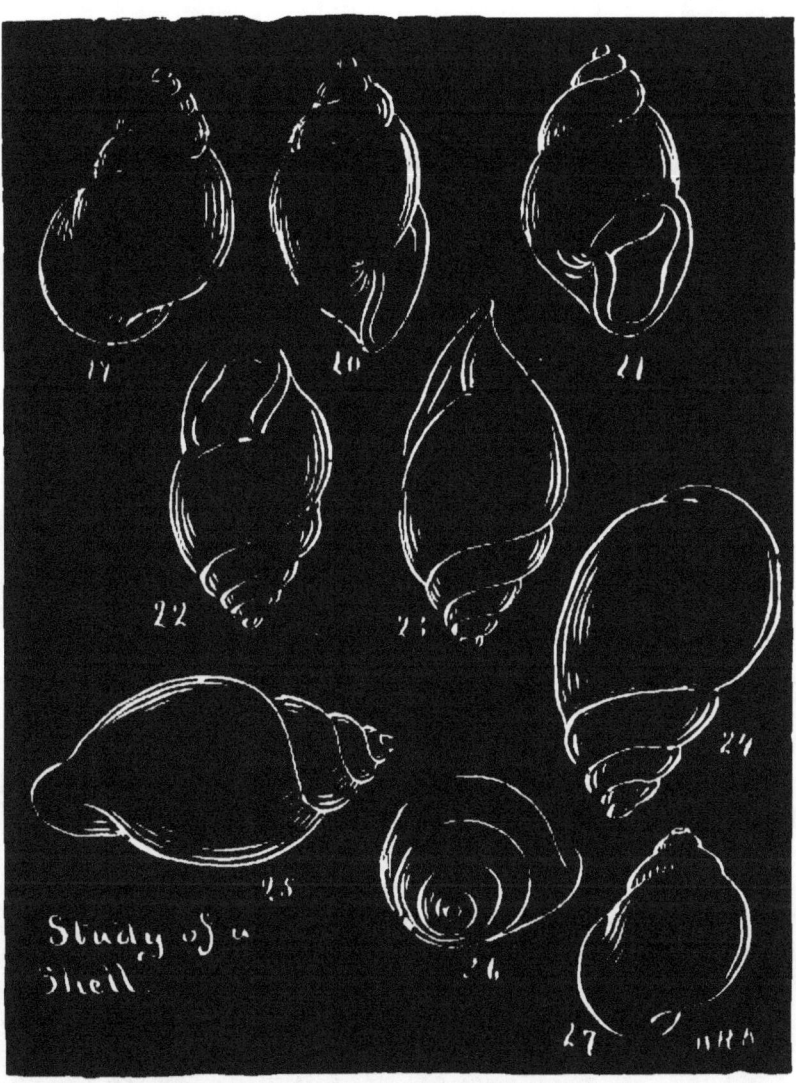

Study of a Shell

show how this may be done. Care must be taken not to carry the device too far. It is perhaps best to use the device without saying anything about it. It should be used toward the close of the lesson.

Shells are both interesting and beautiful, and it is well to have a supply to be used as models for drawing, as well as for other purposes. Perhaps there is no other available object that contains such perfect proportion combined with such beautiful and graceful lines.

Figs. 19-27 represent the same shell drawn in many positions. This is the way all objects should be studied and drawn. It is better to draw one object seven times than seven objects one time.

It is not necessary for each pupil to have the same kind of an object to draw. It is desirable, but not necessary. Excellent work may be done even when each pupil has a different object.

Objects not Suitable for Drawing.—Very few objects are suitable to learn to draw from. Those that are not suitable are: (1) Decorated objects; (2) delicately formed and finished objects; (3) complicated objects.

The decorations on an object tend to draw the attention from the form and thus to confuse the mind of the pupil. Finely formed and finished objects have necessitated a high degree of skill to construct them, and require much the same skill to reproduce them in drawing; and complicated objects are confusing and difficult to understand.

Objects Suitable for Drawing.—In general, objects suitable for drawing are: (1) Plain and simple objects; (2) crudely-formed objects; (3) old and broken objects; (4) natural objects.

Plain and simple objects are easy to understand, which is a

strong factor in their successful reproduction. Crudely-formed objects have required little skill to fashion them, and in consequence are easier to reproduce in drawing. Old and broken objects are more interesting than new and whole objects. Much of their skilled accuracy is worn away and the interesting element of use is seen to better advantage; besides, they are comparatively easy of reproduction.

Small Objects that are Suitable to Hold in One Hand and Draw with the Other.—Key, end of pencil, pen, clothes' peg, fish-hook, sinker, feather, wing, bird's tail, shears, scissors, top, knife, button-hook, pin, tack, nail, screw, pincers, corkscrew, pistol, needle, cup, mug, pipe, tooth-brush, hair-brush, padlock, book, swivel, three chain links, buckle, spool, ink, paste or mucilage bottle.

Box-elder seeds, ash seeds, milkweed pods, ear of corn, wheat, rye, barley and oat heads, acorns, horse-chestnuts, oak galls, peppers, clusters of walnuts, peach stones, gourd, tomato, onion, cucumber, turnip, potato, eggplant, carrot, apples, pears, quinces, peaches, grapes, plums, sweet-peas, poppies, golden-rod, wax balls, rosebuds, roses, chrysanthemums, cosmos, asters and sunflowers, fir cones, pine cones, holly, birds' nests, wasps' nests, cocoanuts, bananas, lemons, lilac buds, horse-chestnut buds, catkins, leaves, grasses, roots, flower buds, dandelion, pansies, violets, apple, peach and cherry blossoms, tulips, crocus, daffodil, radishes, cherries, strawberries, currants, gooseberries.

Cannot Draw All.—It is not necessary to reproduce all the ideas that the object contains. This is usually impossible. We cannot draw all we see, nor is it desirable that we should. We use the model or object to get ideas of form, of size, of relation, of construction; and then represent as many of these ideas as is desired. Of the myriad of ideas that each object possesses we choose those we wish to express—to represent, and no more. We have the power and the right to omit all we do not wish to appear in our drawing.

In the maple seeds, Figs. 28–30, there were many little details that could be seen, there were hundreds of little veins and pores that the eye could easily detect, but as they were not wanted, they were rejected, and only a few veinlets suggested.

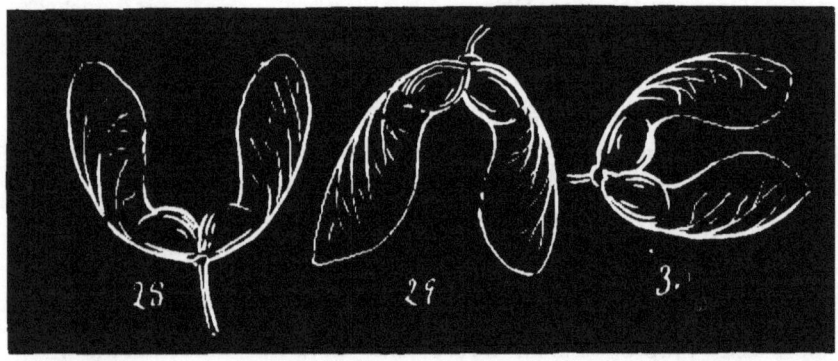

Use the Model Constantly and persistently. The model is the source of the mental image which the pupil reproduces—the source of the idea. If the model is not used then the source of growth is cut off and the pupil uses the same old image over and over again.

Memory Drawing.—The object is *the source*, the drawing is *the how*, and memory drawing is *the test*.

Memory drawing is the test of what the pupil knows of the object. After the model has been studied, test the knowledge by a memory drawing, the same as a test is made in language.

Draw and study the maple seed, Figs. 28–30, and then test the knowledge by drawing the seed from memory. The imagina-

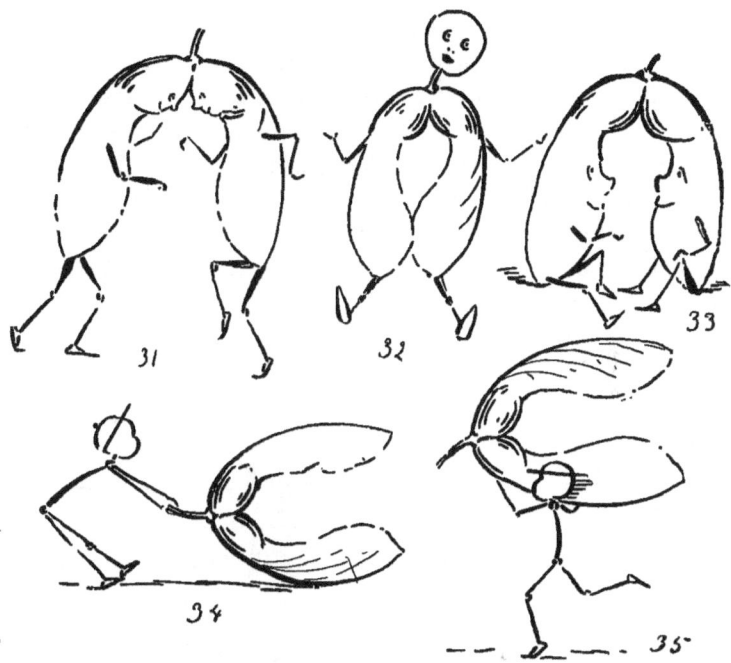

tion may also be used in these tests as in Figs. 31-35, which represent devices that may be used in connection with the seeds to make them interesting, as well as adding life and zest to the drawing.

Drawing Large Objects.—Holding objects in one hand and drawing them with the other, necessarily confines the objects to a size such as can easily be held in one hand. When drawing larger objects, such as a pumpkin, basket, or anything too large to be held in the hand, then the following plan may be followed.

1. Have four boards made that will reach across the aisle from seat to seat, as in Fig. 36. *These boards must be made level.* This may be done by placing books under the edges, but a better

108   AUGSBURG'S DRAWING.

way is to nail a cork or cleat to the under face of each end so that it will be level when placed on the slanting surface of the desk.

2. Place the object or objects to be drawn on these boards.

3. Place the pupils that occupy these seats across which the boards are placed, either at the blackboard to draw objects in their hands, or they may be placed in vacant seats. All is ready now for work. This plan will necessitate the use of four objects, or four groups of objects. It is not necessary that the objects should be alike.

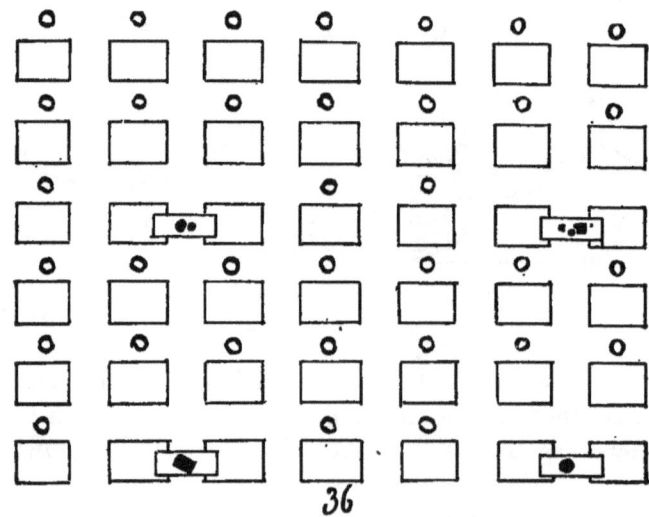

Accent.— Children in general use only one kind of line when drawing, and this line is light or heavy according to the temperament of the child. Children must be taught to use a variety of lines in their drawing.

The use of one line alone is monotonous; it is like singing in only one tone, or talking without modulating the voice. Children must be taught to use light lines and heavy lines; fine gray lines, and broad gray lines; fine black lines and broad black lines;

graded lines; broken lines; lines to express all the varying phases of thought.

Line Accent.— Accent in drawing is very much like accent in talking, and both are and should be caused by the same force — *thought.* Thought causes the modulation of the voice in talking, and thought should cause the modulation of the line in drawing. It is not interesting to talk in a monotone and it is as uninteresting to draw with only one kind of a line.

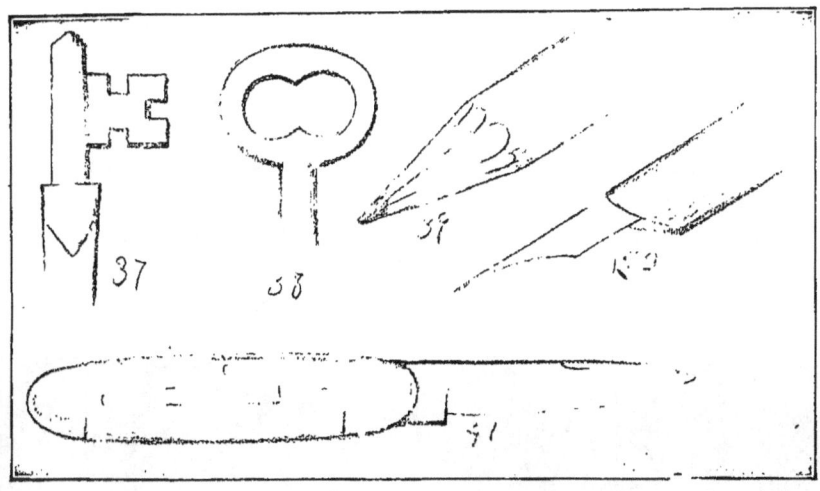

There are two conventional rules that govern line accent, both of which, to some extent, are observable in nature. They are:
1. Accent the right hand and under lines. Figs. 37 and 38.
2. Accent the nearest lines.

But a higher and better way is to *accent the line in such a manner as to bring out your own thought.*

By giving freedom in accent the progress at first will be less, but in the end it will be more rapid and of a higher quality. Figs. 39, 40, and 41 are examples of thought accent.

110 AUGSBURG'S DRAWING.

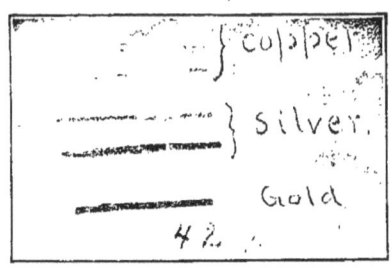

An excellent plan to teach a variety of line is to divide lines into three kinds, as follows:

Three light lines, which for convenience are called *copper*.

Two medium lines, which are called *silver*, and one heavy line which is called *gold*. Require the pupils to use all of these lines in every drawing.

It will be found that by naming the lines copper, silver, and gold, that work can be very easily criticised. The teacher can say of a pupil's drawing, "You have used only copper lines in

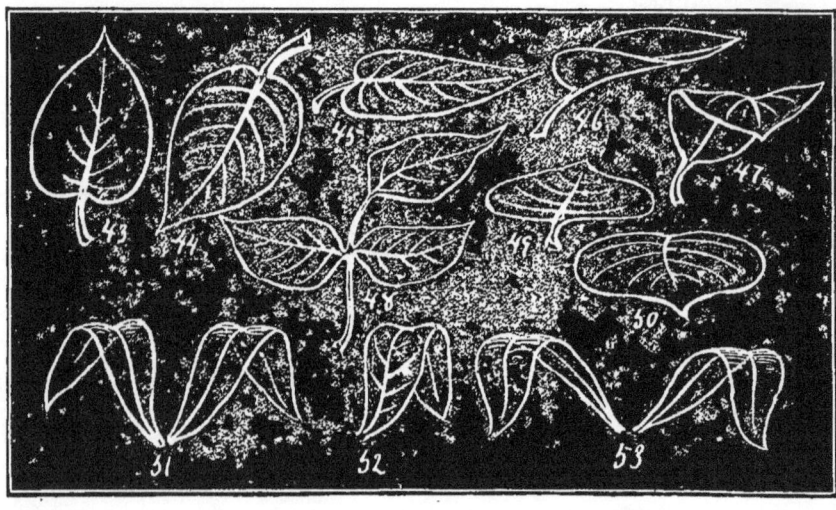

your drawing. Where are the silver and gold?" or, "I do not see the copper and silver lines."

The aim is to make the range of line as wide as possible.

It is better to study an object and gain some degree of proficiency in representing it, than to skip from object to object

ing it in many ways, as the leaf in Figs. 43–53, than to study many different objects with a less degree of thoroughness.

Forming Collections. — Beginning at about the third grade, there is a strong desire on the part of pupils to *collect* — to form collections of marbles, bits of ribbons, postage stamps, minerals, shells, etc. This strong desire for collecting things may be utilized in the drawing class by making a *collection of the drawings of a class of objects* in place of the object itself. For example, to make a drawing of all the various kinds of head-wear, such as hats, caps, helmets, turbans, head-dresses of all descriptions, nations, and tribes, both modern and historical. In doing this begin with the cloak-room and extend to the museum, and lastly to pictures. Lead the pupil to the real object as much as possible.

Pupils will take more interest in collecting, if they have a blank book in which to place or paste the drawings after they are made.

The following objects are excellent to form lines of collecting:

seeds	nuts	vegetables	leaves
fruits	houses	barns	keys
wagons	cans	pitchers	cups
vases	knives	axes	bridges
boats	head-wear	foot-wear	chairs, etc.

Figs. 54–70 show a collection of head-wear. This list could be extended into the hundreds.

DRILL EXERCISES.

This drill exercise is merely to suggest lines of work and kinds of objects that might, perhaps, be overlooked by the teacher.

1. Mary, show me how the end of my key looks, by means of a drawing. (Either on blackboard or tablet.)

2. Paul, show me, by means of a drawing, how you have sharpened your pencil.

3. Show how your pen fits into the pen-holder.

4. Is that a new knife you have, Henry? Make a drawing of it on the blackboard.

5. Is that a peanut you have, Jane? Make a drawing of it on your tablet.

6. Stand at the window, Peter, and draw that tree yonder.

7. Children, watch this milkweed seed as I blow it into the air. Make a drawing of it as it appears in the air.

8. I will hang this hat on a pointer. Each one make a drawing of it.

9. This afternoon we will close school twenty minutes early, and draw the big tree in the corner of the yard.

10. Who can bring sixty milkweed pods to school to-morrow? Henry and George may bring them. Pick them with long stems and stalks and we will use them for a drawing lesson.

11. To-morrow the circus is coming to town. I would like Charles, Henry, Allen, James, and Paul to make a drawing of the tent, on paper, and then reproduce it on the blackboard.

12. Abner has made such a funny Jack-o'-Lantern; I will place it here where all can see it. Each make a drawing of it.

13. Are the violets out so soon? Thank you for this bunch. Let each of us take one and see if we can make a drawing of it in three positions.

14. This old canteen was carried through the war by Mr. James. (Story.) I will hang it up here where we can make a drawing of it.

15. The last hour on Friday afternoon we will visit that old deserted stone house and make a drawing of it.

16. Mary, you may be excused to draw the stump yonder. Susie, the fence corner. Edna, the gate, and Julia, the old apple tree.

17. The following are good groups to place on the boards that are placed across the aisles :

>Pumpkin and gourd.
>Pumpkin and squash.
>Three turnips.
>Turnips and basket.
>Turnips, kettle, and knife.
>Tomatoes and bowl.
>Three apples.
>Three pears.
>Three carrots.
>Apple, pear, and lemon.
>A cluster of nuts on a limb.
>A pear on a limb with leaves.
>A simple plant in its pot.
>Teapot and cup.
>Three flowers in a vase or bottle.

18. Make a collection of the drawings of leaves.
19. Make a collection of the drawings of keys.
20. Make a collection of the drawings of knives.
21. Make a collection of the drawings of pitchers.
22. Make a collection of the drawings of foot-wear

CHAPTER X.

QUICK DRAWING.

The aim in this chapter is to show how to draw rapidly, and n the most direct manner, any object or idea the teacher may wish to represent.

The Idea.—An idea is the strongest and quickest force in the world, and consumes in its representation comparatively little time. *Ignorance* is the negative element of the idea, and is the weakest and slowest condition in the world, and the great time consumer.

The idea, then, is the great propelling force in drawing and must be *first*.

Suggestion.—The chief hand maid of the idea is suggestion. Next to the idea, suggestion is the most important word in drawing. If rightly used it can do more work, save more time and accomplish greater results, than any other word.

In drawing, we cannot represent everything we see; we must discriminate between the very few essentials and the many non-essentials. There are thousands of little details that must be rejected, there are dozens of accessories that need only to be suggested, and there is usually only one idea that must be represented.

For example, the idea is a rabbit, Fig. 1, which is represented as directly and with as few lines as possible. There are hundreds of little details about the rabbit which are not represented—spots, fur, color, light, shade, are all rejected because the idea in its simplest form is wanted. Surrounding the rabbit there

AUGSBURG'S DRAWING.

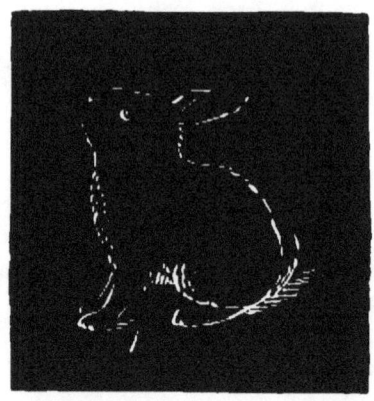

may be many accessories, twigs, leaves, grasses, pebbles, etc., but as they are not needed in connection with the central idea — the rabbit — they are also rejected.

The point is this: we are not bound by the number of details and accessories that exist, but simply by those we wish to introduce into our drawing to make our idea as complete as we wish to have it. The object we are drawing has no power to dictate to us and say how much or how little we shall represent of it. This is determined solely by the desire of the draughtsman; light, shade, shadows, details, accessories are our servants, not our masters.

How to Use the Idea.—The following rule or law will show how, in a general way, to use the idea in drawing:

Connect the mind with the idea or object you wish to represent by means of its leading features or characteristics, and when the connection is made, stop.

For example, suppose one wishes to represent a hat. What is the leading feature of a hat? A moment's thought will convince us that it is the rim. Supply this to almost any shaped form for a crown and a hat is the result. The band also, is a prominent characteristic.

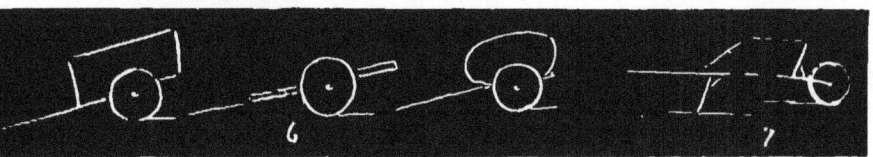

Suppose we wish to represent a cart. What is the leading feature of a cart? What makes a cart a cart? You will see at once that it is *the two wheels*. If these are added or suggested to almost any kind of a form, the idea *cart* will be represented as in Fig. 6. The leading feature of a wagon is *four wheels*. The leading features of a wheel-barrow are four in number, *one wheel, handles, back and legs*, Fig. 7.

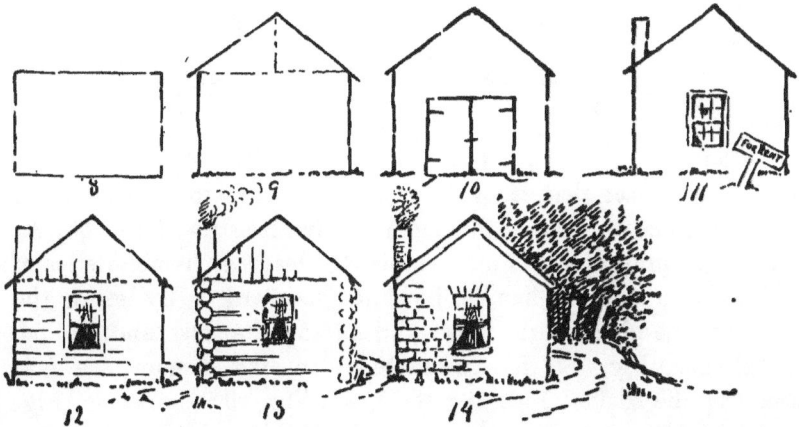

The leading feature of a house is the roof. Attach a roof to any regular form, such as Fig. 8, and a house is suggested, as Fig.

9. Big doors are the leading features of a barn, Fig. 10. A window and chimney suggest a dwelling house, Fig. 11. The curtains in the window suggest that somebody is living in the house, Fig. 12. The smoke coming out of the chimney suggests that the people are at home, Fig. 13. Fig. 12 suggests that the house is made of boards, Fig. 13 of logs, Fig. 14 of stone. It is not necessary or desirable to place the boards, logs or stone all over the side of the house. This would emphasize this feature too much, besides the eye does not see at the same time in more than one place. It does not see all. It sees only what is cognized by the mind.

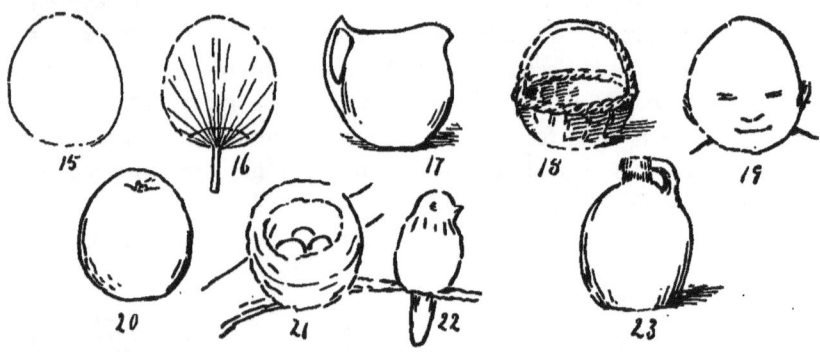

Choose a common form, say an oval, Fig. 15. Think of most any object that is oval, or may be made to appear in an oval form, and by adding the leading characteristics of the object, it can be represented. For example, the leading characteristics of a pitcher are its nose, handle, bowl and standard. By letting the oval take the place of the bowl and adding the nose and handle, the pitcher, Fig. 17, is represented. In like manner, the fan, Fig. 16; the basket, Fig. 18; the head, Fig. 19; the apple, Fig. 20; the bird's nest, Fig. 21; the bird, Fig. 22; the jug, Fig. 23; as well as many other objects may be represented.

Animals also, may be represented in the same manner; Figs. 40-45 are a number of circular forms to which are added the leading features of several common animals.

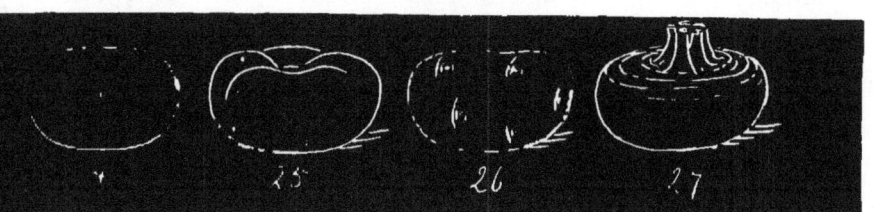

We speak of a line as having expression, and of lines being full of expression, or expressing this or that quality, when in reality the line, in itself, has no expression that is not imparted to it by thought. Thought is the vitalizing principle, and without it the line is nothing. The line is merely the expression of the thought, the medium through which the thought is made visible.

Fig. 24 is merely a form with no definite idea back of it. It is nothing as near as it is possible to represent nothing with a line. Now add to this form, lines that do represent ideas and they will be recognized at once, as in Figs. 25, 26 and 27.

It is not the lines that represent these objects, but the idea— the thought back of these lines.

Between the beginning and the end of the drawing, there is no end. There has never been a drawing made so perfect that it could not be made more perfect. There has never been a pictur so beautiful that it could not be made more beautiful. If then, there is no end—no point beyond which it is impossible to go, then we have the privilege of stopping anywhere we wish and calling the drawing complete, when the idea we wish to represent is complete. For example, it is quite impossible to represent all the details of a landscape. How much shall we represent? *What we wish and no more.* If we wish simply a landscape, a tree, Fig. 28, is enough to suggest one; or a hill, river or pond will do the same. A landscape may be suggested by anything a landscape contains. As the hill, road, tree, in Fig. 29, or the wigwams, etc., in Fig. 30.

It is not necessary to place in the landscape everything; to do this is impossible, but only as much as the draughtsman wishes to convey in expressing his thought.

Glass is very puzzling to represent if we try to imitate it exactly as it appears to the eye. But if we look at it through its characteristics, it is very simple. What are the leading characteristics of glass? *Transparency* is the most important, and *reflection* is next. Represent these two qualities and glass is at once suggested. Transparency is represented by *showing something through*, and reflection by reflecting usually light in the form of what is called high light. The rectangular plane in Fig. 32 is opaque, in Fig. 33 it is made transparent by showing the post through it. The tumbler, Fig. 31, is made transparent by showing the further line of the bottom, and the high light on the further side of the tumbler.

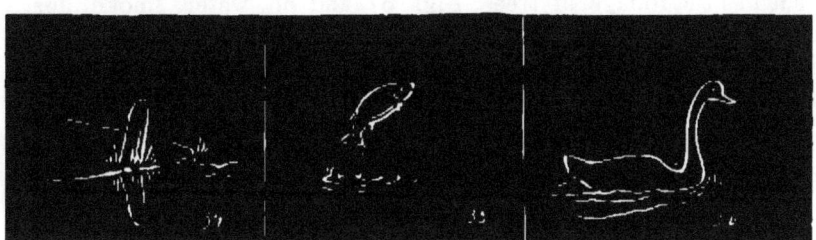

Still water is without form; how then can it be represented? We can do it by connecting the mind with the space we wish the water to occupy, by means of something that will suggest water. In Fig. 34 the post and bird do not suggest water, but their *reflection* does, because one of the chief characteristics of still water is its power to reflect. In Fig. 35, the fish does not suggest water, but the fish *jumping* does. In Fig. 36, the swan does not suggest water, but the swan *swimming* does. A horse will not suggest water, but a horse *drinking*, *swimming*, or *wading*, will. A boy will not suggest water, but a boy *fishing*, *diving*, *floating* or *rowing*, will. The object itself does not suggest water, but its *action* may.

Invisible forces, such as air and light, can be represented by their effect on visible objects. We look out of doors and say the wind blows, or the air is still, by its effect on unstable substances, such as the foliage of trees, Figs. 37 and 38, water, smoke, dust, bunting, etc.

We say the sun shines, by its effect on visible objects, making one side light and leaving the other darker, as in Fig. 39. Many artists depend largely on representing different phases of light, for the chief beauty of their picture.

39

The Spiritual.— Now we are coming to the representation of that which has neither form nor color, that which is without visible appearance or tangible shape, that which the eye cannot see, nor the ear hear, and yet, which is higher, more important, more powerful, more real, and more lasting, than all other qualities — the representation of the spiritual.

Many, if not all visible objects, have a double meaning — their material and symbolic meaning,— which is more or less recognized. The spiritual is represented through these higher or symbolic meanings. For example, an anchor is used to drop to the bottom of the sea to keep the vessel from drifting, or being blown about by the wind; but when an anchor is chiseled on a monument, it becomes the symbol of hope, which is its spiritual meaning.

In the same manner, the key is the symbol of knowledge; the sword of truth; and the crown of honor.

The following are symbols that may be used with profit in the school-room:

Lamp — learning	Olive branch — peace
Reed — weakness	Rock — constancy
Shackles — bondage	Star — promise
Fountain — source	Sun — Creator
Cross — victory, trials	Torch — anarchy or learning
Altar — sacrifice	Rainbow — promise
Grapes — fruitfulness	Harp — praise
Beehive — industry	Scales — justice
Hour-glass — time	Lily — purity

Ark — safety

In the same manner many birds and animals have been symbolized or made typical of qualities that are generally recognized:

Dove — gentleness	Owl — wisdom
Hawk — voracity	Ox — patience
Horse — strength	Tiger — ferocity
Hog — greed	Serpent — sin
Mule — stubbornness	Lion — dignity

DRILL EXERCISES.

Represent in drawing, by means of their leading features and characteristics, the following objects:

A bowl	A barrel	A rubber overshoe
A teapot	A basket	A hammer
A pitcher	An umbrella	A saw
A jug	A hat	A wrench
An oil can	A cap	A mallet
A flower-pot	A slipper	A book
A pail	A shoe	A valise
A drum	A horn.	A flag

A sled	A cart	A broom
A brush	A skate	A key
A fish-hook	A mug	A feather
A padlock	An ear of corn	An acorn
A pumpkin	A squash	A tomato
An onion	A cucumber	A turnip
A potato	A cherry	A tree
A pine tree	A poplar tree	An elm tree
A palm tree	A barn	A shed
A cabin	A house	A tent
An island	A peninsula	A lake
	Still water	

CHAPTER XI.

THE DRAWING OF BIRDS.

In drawing, all objects should be studied under the general heads of:

The Copy, or Imitation.
The Object, or Observation.
The Memory and Imagination.

In general, these three divisions should go hand in hand, each helping to explain and make clear the others. But if an order is followed in the study of birds, the best one for young pupils is as follows: (1) The copy; (2) memory and imagination; (3) the object.

This order, however, is not intended to be arbitrary. If the object is something that can be leisurely studied, like a leaf, or a flower, then an order similar to this should be followed: (1) The object; (2) the copy; (3) memory and imagination.

Birds.—The principle of the construction of all birds is, in general, the same; the difference is in the proportion and minor details. By learning the proportions and general features from pictures and drawings, much time will be saved, and the work made more effective and less discouraging than if the study is attempted from the living bird alone. This does not mean to blindly copy the drawings of others, but to study them intelligently, to study them with a view of learning their form and proportion and the general principle of bird construction. To learn such points

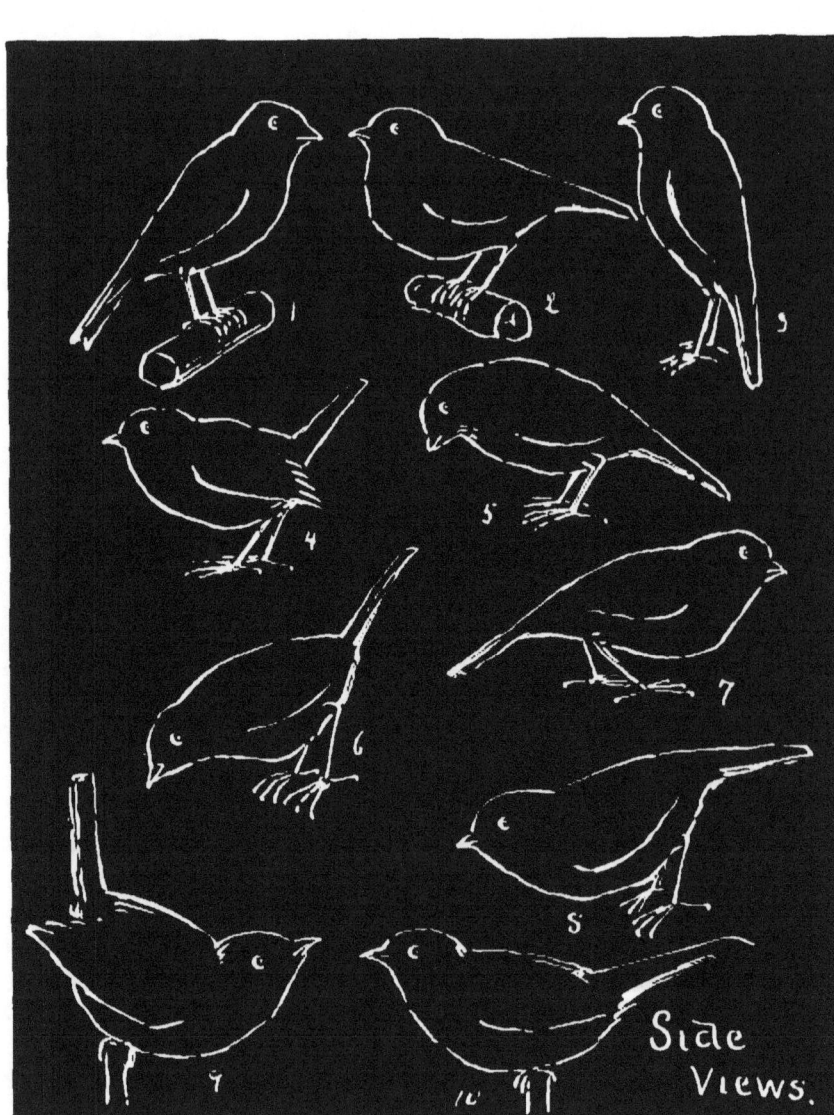

Side Views.

as the following: The size of the head as compared with the body; the movements of the tail, head and body; how the feet are placed under the body to give perfect balance; how the wings rest on the body, and their movements when flying. All of these can be studied from drawings coupled with observation, and then verified on the real bird, much better than from the real bird alone. It is doubtful if one untrained in drawing can make very much headway learning to draw from such a restless bit of animation as a live bird, with its multiplicity of markings and numberless details. One must have both knowledge of the bird and skill in drawing to do this.

Balance.— A bird's feet must be under the middle of the body — that is, the center of gravity must fall within the area of the feet. A bird cannot stand up, any more than a human being, if the feet are not under the center of the body. *The body must be balanced on the feet.* In Figs. 1–10, if a vertical line is passed through the center of the body it will pass between or within the area of the feet. In Figs. 8 and 9 the center of the bird is in front of the feet, and the bird has the appearance of falling forward as if ready to spring.

Character.— Character is more than accuracy in drawing. We cannot represent all. Choose, therefore, between those details which are essential and which characterize the bird, and those which are of little importance. The *idea* you are representing is the great essential. This should always be first. What am I drawing? what idea am I representing? what is my object and aim in this drawing? — are questions that cannot be too plainly answered.

AUGSBURG'S DRAWING.

Divisions of Study.—For convenience, the study of the bird may be divided into — 1. Side views; 2. Front views; 3. Back views; 4. Quarter views; 5. Flying. While the study of the bird in these various positions is an aid in their representation, giving variety of position and mechanical channels of thought, still, it is the idea back of these devices that is the vital force. These positions are merely mechanical aids, and are attendant to and subordinate to the idea. If you wish to represent a bird singing, they say, *You can represent a bird singing in various positions; among the most prominent are the side, front, back, and quarter views.*

General Directions.— *Draw the large part of the bird first.* The body is the largest part. It is easier to add the smaller parts — such as the head, tail, and legs — to the body, than to add the the body to these smaller parts. Work from the large to the small, from the mass to the details, from the general to the special.

Sketch the bird with light lines to get the general proportion and action, as shown in Fig. 58, and then finish in detail. Be sure the *proportion, balance,* and *action* of the bird are correct before finishing the drawing. By *proportion* is meant the proper relative size of body, head, tail, and legs. By *balance* is meant standing firm and stable, without the feeling that the bird will fall backwards or forwards. This balance may be secured by passing a vertical line through the center of the body in such a manner as to fall between or within the area of the feet. By correct *action* is meant making the bird appear to be doing what you intend it to do; such as flying, eating, singing, etc., as in Figs. 61-70.

Learn the *limitations* of each part of the bird. For example, the tail may be elevated or depressed, as in Fig. 54; and it may be closed up or spread out like a fan, as in Figs. 59 and 60.

The head has a vertical range, greater than is pictured in Fig. 55, and on a pivot of at least one complete revolution, Fig. 54. The combination of these two movements enables the bird to practically place its head in any position. The body also has movements on the legs that are both lateral and vertical.

Figs. 56 and 57 show the principal positions of the wings when flying.

The idea, being the strongest force in drawing, should also be the propelling force in all of this work. The following general outline will be found an orderly and progressive method of study:

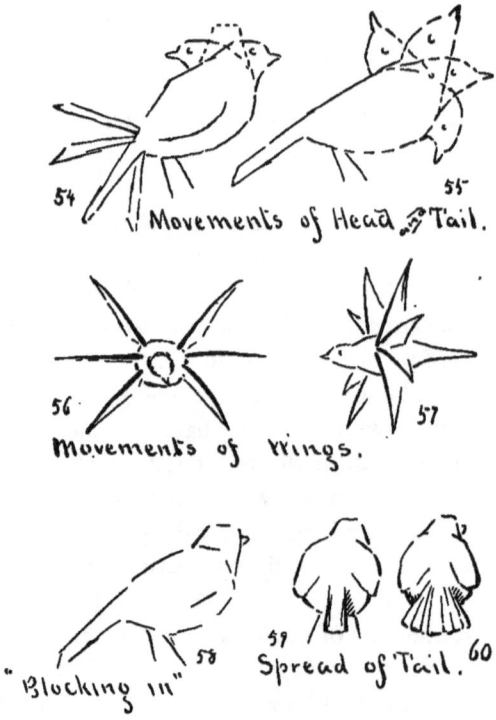

1. Draw the various positions side view.
2. Draw the various positions front view.
3. Draw the various positions back view.
4. Draw the various positions quarter view.
5. Draw the various positions flying.

The following sources for the study of the bird may be mentioned: 1. Drawings; 2. Pictures of birds; 3. Mounted specimens; 4. The living bird.

Figs. 61–70 represent what is meant by making the *idea* prominent in each drawing. In each one of these the bird is

AUGSBURG'S DRAWING.

represented as *doing* something. This is better and much more interesting than simply drawing a bird. The element *interest* is the greatest incentive to progress. There is little or no progress if the minds of the pupils are passive, however much they may be urged by the teacher. *Busy-ness* is not necessarily progress. A pupil may be *busy* drawing, and his mind passive;

especially is this true in drawing lessons twenty or thirty minutes long. Twelve minutes is about the right length of time. This will give one minute to get ready, one minute to close, and ten minutes for drawing. Long lessons are tiresome to pupils. If explanation and instruction are necessary, add three minutes more, making fifteen minutes in all.

I sometimes scold the naughty crows.

By making the idea the prominent part in the drawing, interest is at once awakened and progress carried on much more rapidly than can possibly be done otherwise. If a child tries to represent a bird singing, and is not entirely successful, he will be very apt to watch the next bird he sees, in order to perfect his image of the bird in the act of singing.

It looks like rain we must preen our feathers.

AUGSBURG'S DRAWING.   135

Figs. 71–79 represent a swimming bird—the duck—doing the various things a duck will do during his daily round of life. These drawings are given as an example to show how any bird may be studied. Figs. 61–70 are given as examples for any of the common birds, and Figs. 71–79 for any swimming bird. In like manner any of the following birds may be studied:

Common birds — swallow, cedar bird, sparrow, lark, oriole, bobolink, crow, jay, kingfisher, wood-pecker, robin, and blue-bird.

Birds of prey — hawk, eagle, buzzard, owl, osprey.

Swimming birds — duck, swan, goose, loon, pelican, and gull.

Wading birds — crane, stork, woodcock, and snipe.

DRILL EXERCISES.

1. Draw a bird, side view, looking up.
2. Draw a bird, side view, looking down.
3. Draw a bird, side view, sleeping.
4. Draw a bird, side view, sitting on a limb.
5. Draw a bird, side view, building its nest.
6. Draw a bird, side view, sitting on its nest.
7. Draw a bird, side view, singing.
8. Draw a bird, side view, eating.
9. Draw a bird, side view, drinking.
10. Draw a bird, side view, scolding.
11. Draw a bird, side view, preening its feathers.
12. Draw a bird, side view, sharpening its bill.
13. Draw a bird, side view, pulling a worm from the ground.
14. Draw a bird, side view, bathing.
15. Draw a bird, side view, flying.

Note.—The above actions and as many more as are desirable, should be repeated in (1) front view; (2) back view; (3) in any of the four quarter views.

16. Draw a bird flying, side view. Front view. Back view. Quarter view. Flying upward. Downward. To the right. To the left.
17. Draw three birds on a limb, front, back, and quarter views.
18. Draw three birds on the ground, side, front, and back views.

In like manner these examples may be multiplied indefinitely.

CHAPTER XII.

The Drawing of Animals.

The General Plan for the study of animals is as follows:

1. Study and learn one animal thoroughly.
2. Use the knowledge thus acquired in the study of all animals.

The Cat as a Type.— Of all animals, the cat is the best as well as the most available animal to make the basis of study. This is not because of her domestic relation to us so much as on account of her uniform size, appearance, and accessibility. Children generally are better acquainted with the cat than with any other animal.

The dog and the rabbit are also excellent models, and if more convenient may be used in place of the cat.

The general plan for the study of the cat or other animal is as follows:

Through imitation or the copy.
Through observation or the object.
Through memory and imagination.

Imitation Drawing.— Through imitation or the copy the relative size and position of the parts, the details, and general facts of the animal are best learned. It is possible to learn these

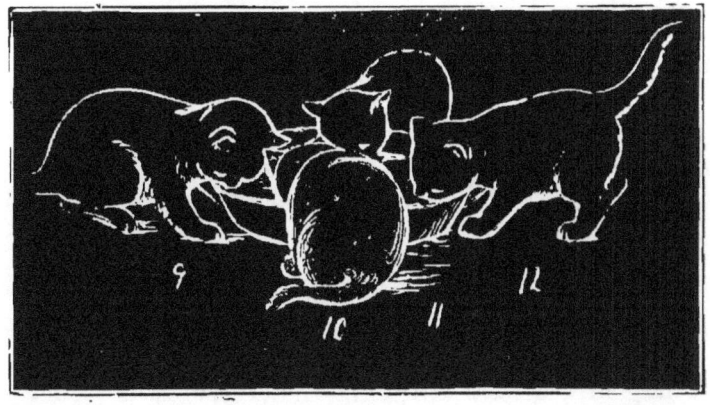

facts directly from the live animal, but it is more difficult and not nearly as convenient. The drawing or copy is at rest and admits of close study in one position; the animal is restless and will not remain quiet long enough for an untrained pupil to sketch or draw it. The copy contains both the idea and how to represent the idea; the animal represents the idea only, and there is nothing to show how to represent it on a flat surface. The copy is convenient for use in the class-room; the animal is so inconvenient that few teachers will even attempt its study.

The aim, then, in copying the different positions of the cat, is:

1. To learn the form and position of each part.
2. To learn the relative size and proportion of each part.
3. To learn how to represent the animal on a flat surface.

Blind copying without a worthy end in view, is as wrong in drawing as in language. Copying alone is incomplete; it is merely the first step toward learning to represent animals, and should be followed by both the study of the real animal, and tested by imagination and memory drawing.

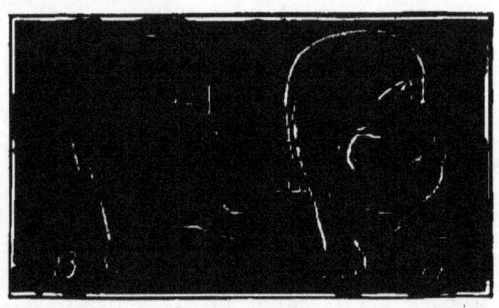

Study of the Real Animal.— After the facts about the animal have been learned, such as the relative size of each part, the shape of the ear, head, body, and legs, then all of these can be verified on the real animal. This may be done by bringing a pet cat or kitten into the school-room and keeping it there until it feels at home, then drawings may be made from it at such times as opportunity presents. A better plan, however, is to encourage pupils to draw from the animal at home, and then bring their drawing to the school, thus encouraging independent work. Such drawings should be copied or drawn from memory on the blackboard, by way of encouragement.

Imaginative or Memory Drawing is the fruit of the study from both the copy and the object. It is the pupil's expression of what he knows about the animal or object he is studying — the guage of what he really possesses — the index to the power he has to express, and as such should be of common use.

These three divisions — imitation, observation, and imagination — are given in a definite order, but in practice they merge into each other at every point. The copy, the object, and the memory test should be of mutual help in acquiring a mastery over the common object.

Similarity of Animals.— Animals are very much alike in the general principle of their construction. All of them have a body, head, ears, tail, and legs, that are alike in plan, but differ in size, proportion, and minor details. Examine the hind leg of a cat, for example, and it will be found very similar to the hind leg of a mouse, a squirrel, a sheep, a cow, a horse, or a lion. The difference being so slight in the general principle that the learning of one will be found the key to all the others. The same similarity will be found in the other parts of the animals as well, so much so that the thorough understanding of the drawing of one animal becomes the basis of the drawing of all animals.

Plan of Drawing.— Draw the large parts first. It is easier and better to add the small parts to the large than it is to reverse the order.

The general plan is about as follows:

1. With light lines mark in the general shape of the body, as in Figs. 18–22.
2. With a light line mark in the general shape of the head.
3. Lightly mark in the legs and the tail.
4. Finish.

Often, as in Figs. 18 and 22, it may be best to block in the head first. but in general the plan above will be found good.

Mass and Details.— The mass is of more importance than the details. Children, naturally, when drawing, see the details — the little parts, first; they must be taught to see the large parts. This may be done as in Chapter VIII., by teaching the simple geometrical forms, and then leading the pupils to see these forms in the object they are drawing. For example, in Fig. 23, to

recognize that the head and body are circular, is a great aid in reproducing these large parts in right proportion. A recognition of the circle and oval in Fig. 24, will do the same.

Material for Work.— Collect from magazines, books, papers, and whatever other sources at command, pictures and drawings of cats in all sorts of positions. Trim the pictures to convenient size and paste them neatly on stiff cardboard. Arrange these pictures into convenient groups, showing like elements, to be learned, such as:

The side view, Figs. 25-28.
The front view, Figs. 29-32.
Quarter views, Figs. 33-35.
Lying down positions, Figs. 36-46.

These divisions into groups showing like difficulties to be overcome, are also a great aid in indicating the position desired

when dictating to the class a given position, such as a cat eating, side view, front view, back view, etc., Figs. 9–12.

If one particular position is desired for the whole class, then this position may be carefully drawn on the blackboard for the whole class to study, or it may be reproduced by means of a hectograph, and each pupil have a copy.

Office of the Line.— It is the office of the line to show direction. The direction of the line is of more importance than the quality of the line. The poorest line indicating right direction is better than the most beautiful line in the wrong direction. *Direction is more than line.*

Character is a higher quality than technical accuracy. Character is interesting, technical accuracy is cold and of very little interest to children. If necessary, sacrifice technical accuracy for character.

148   AUGSBURG'S DRAWING.

The Thought.— The idea is the strongest propelling force that can be placed back of the drawing. Write down the various positions and actions of the cat that represent definite ideas or thoughts, such as:

Eating	Drinking	Sitting	Running
Walking	Creeping	Washing face	Jumping
Sleeping	Rolling	Washing body	Watching
Mewing	Climbing	Washing paws	Catching
		Playing	

Make the idea you wish represented as vivid and strong as possible.

The Illustrations.— Figs. 1–8 represent brush drawing, which is taken up fully in Chapter XIV. It is a very suggestive and interesting means of representing animals.

AUGSBURG'S DRAWING.   149

Figs. 9–12 show the four principal positions of the cat. By learning these positions we extend our knowledge so we can represent any position.

Figs. 13 and 14 and 18–22 show the manner of blocking in

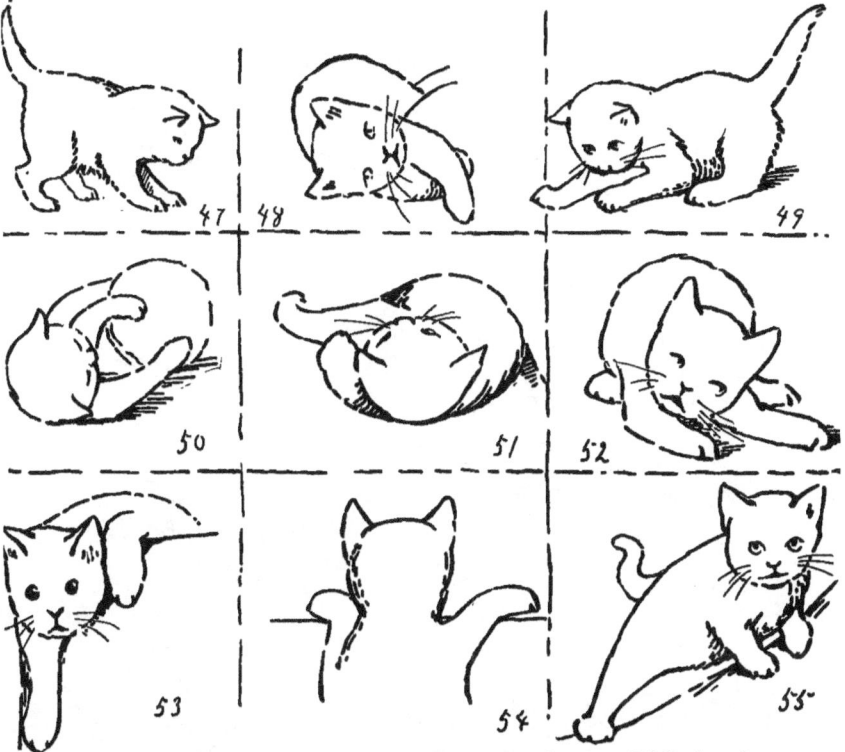

the work to represent the general proportions. This is always done with light lines, so light that they need not be erased.

Figs. 23 and 24 are intended to show how the geometrical figures enter into the reproduction of amimal forms.

Figs. 25–28 represent the side view of a cat. This is the view that children most commonly recognize and represent.

150   AUGSBURG'S DRAWING.

Figs. 29–32 represent the front view of the cat. Observe that the circle predominates in this view.

Figs. 33–35 represent the quarter views; these are the most numerous.

Figs. 36–46 represent some of the lying-down positions. The cat lying down is the most convenient and easiest for first

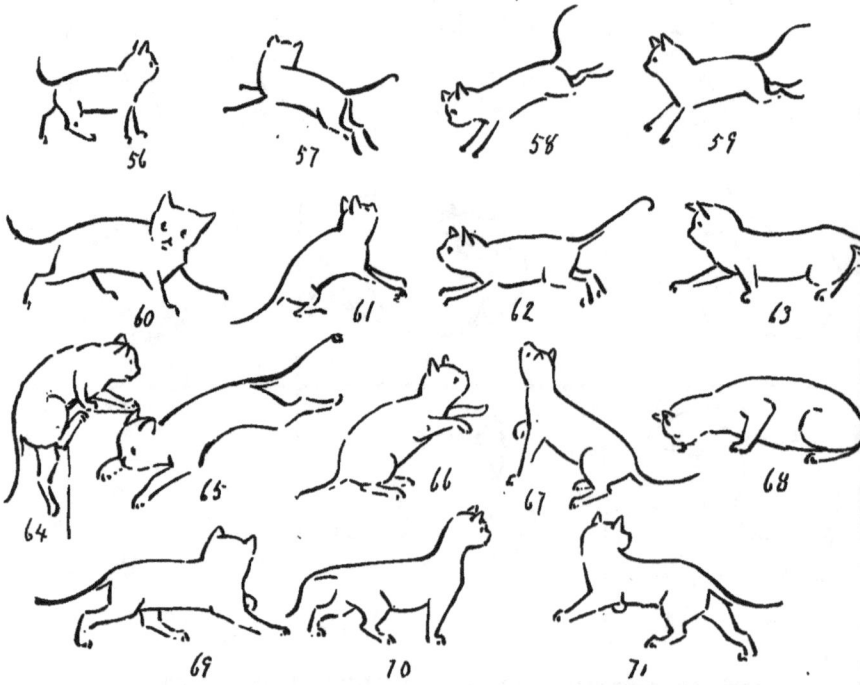

efforts in drawing from the live cat. The positions are not only easier, but the animal will remain quiet for a longer period of time, thus enabling the pupil to make a drawing.

The positions taken by kittens when playing are always interesting, but require much study and knowledge of the cat, as well as persistent practice to catch the movements and place them on paper.

Figs. 56–71 represent some of the characteristic actions of the cat. These actions are represented by the action lines only. All other lines have been omitted.

SUGGESTIVE DRILL EXERCISES.

1. Teach the pupil to "block in" with light lines, their work, as in Fig. 13 before finishing, as in Fig. 14. The best way to do this is to let the pupils see the teacher draw in this manner. At different times draw Figs. 18, 19, 20, 21, and 22 on the blackboard, that the pupils may see how it is done.

2. Study the side view. Draw a cat similar to the side view, Fig. 25. Draw one very carefully on the blackboard where all the pupils can see it plainly. Draw attention to the fact that the head is round and the body, including the legs, is rectangular. Lead the pupils to draw the body — the large parts first, and to this, add the smaller parts, and follow with the details.

3. Make a hectograph copy of Fig. 27 so that each pupil may have a copy. Let the pupils carefully copy this position with a view of reproducing it on the blackboard from memory. Let those who can, draw it on the blackboard from memory.

4. Teach the pupil how to draw Fig. 26 from memory, then have the pupils represent a cat catching a mouse, a bird, or any object that may illustrate this position.

5. Sketch Fig. 29 on the blackboard and ask a pupil to point out the general shape of the head. The body. Ask which part they would draw first. Second. In like manner draw several cats and teach the pupils to recognize the shape of the whole or part.

6. Make a hectograph copy of Figs. 29–32 in such a manner that they can be cut apart and each pupil have one. Let them copy these and draw on the blackboard from memory.

7. Draw Figs. 23 and 24 on the blackboard. Ask for a

recognition of the general shape of the head. Body. Let the pupils draw each one, then reproduce it on the blackboard.

8. Make the pupils familiar with some of the principal positions in the quarter views, by hectograph copies.

9. Lead the pupils to learn some of the principal positions lying down.

10. Procure a cat or kitten. Teach it to make its nest in a convenient place where the pupils can see it, and then let drawings be made as opportunity is given.

11. Draw a cat sleeping, side view. Front view. Back view. Quarter view.

12. Represent a cat eating.
13. Represent a cat drinking.
14. Represent a cat sitting.
15. Represent a cat running.
16. Represent a cat walking.
17. Represent a cat creeping.
18. Represent a cat rolling.
19. Represent a cat jumping.
20. Represent a cat watching.
21. Represent a cat mewing.
22. Represent a cat climbing.
23. Represent a cat playing with a ball.
24. Represent a cat catching a mouse or bird.
25. Represent a cat washing her face.
26. Represent a cat washing her body.
27. Represent a cat washing her paw.
28. Represent a cat listening.

CHAPTER XIII.

Teaching Color.

Materials.— The minimum of material needed for teaching color is:
1. A color chart.
2. Colored papers.
3. Colored material.

1. THE COLOR CHART is the standard of color — the color measure. The basis of the chart is the solar spectrum.

The color charts that may be obtained consist of colored papers representing:
1. The six primary or standard colors, — red, orange, yellow, green, blue and violet.
2. The six primary colors, with two intermediate colors, the first and second tints, and the first and second shades of each.
3. The six primary colors and their complementaries.
4. The broken spectrum scales.
5. The principal grays.

It is well to keep these charts closed when not in use.

2. COLORED PAPERS for teaching color are put up in various styles of packages representing the same colors as those found on the color charts. These papers are used in connection with the chart for the drilling of pupils.

3. COLORED MATERIAL is the various material collected by the teacher and pupils, such as bits of ribbon, worsted, silk, tissue paper, etc., for general color study. It is to be used in connection with the color chart and follows the use of colored papers.

Color Definitions. — STANDARDS are colors which, by common consent, are accepted as types. They are red, orange, yellow, green, blue, and violet, and are based on the solar spectrum.

PURE COLOR is the most intense expression of that color.

A TINT is the same color made lighter.

A SHADE is the same color made darker.

A SINGLE COLOR SCALE is an orderly arrangement of that color through its tints, color, and shades.

A SCALE OF COLORS is an orderly arrangement of related colors. Red, orange, yellow, green, blue, violet, together with their intermediates, form the principal color scale.

A TONE is a step in a color scale.

LUMINOUS COLORS are bright colors. Yellow is the most luminous of colors.

WARM AND COLD COLORS. Colors tending toward orange are called warm; those tending toward blue, cold.

WARM AND COLD GRAYS. Grays tinted with warm color are called warm; those tinted with cold color, cold.

LOCAL COLOR is the natural color of the object, seen under ordinary light.

BROKEN COLORS are colors dulled by grays.

PRESERVING COLORED MATERIAL.

The colored material collected by teacher and pupils may be preserved in seven boxes, marked red, orange, yellow, green, blue, violet, and gray, Fig. 1.

Put all sorts of reds, and material in which red predominates, into the box marked "red," and the same with "orange," and the other colors. This

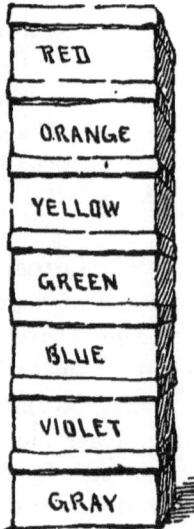

material is invaluable in the study of color. Encourage the pupils to make a color collection of their own.

ORDER OF TEACHING COLOR.

1. Teach all the primary colors, and gray. Do not teach each color separately, but all together. Begin by dividing the color world of the child into seven parts — into red, orange, yellow, green, blue, violet, and gray. In doing this do not discriminate between the colors of each part, but call all reds, *red;* and all yellows, *yellow*, of whatever tint, shade, or hue they may be.

2. Divide each primary color into three parts — into tint, color, and shade. Do not discriminate between different tints and shades of the color, but simply teach the child to recognize the tint of red, the pure red itself, and the shade of red.

3. The full spectrum scale of pure colors.
4. Complementary colors.
5. Warm and cold colors, neutral gray, warm and cold grays.
6. Broken spectrum scales.

METHOD OF TEACHING COLOR.

Teach color by comparison with a color chart.

The following are some of the most simple methods of teaching this subject.

1. Place on a table a number of papers representing the six primary colors. Point to a primary color on the chart and ask a pupil to find it among the papers on the table. Do this with all the colors.

2. Hold up before the class a card with a colored paper pasted to it. Ask a pupil to point to the same color on the color chart. Drill with all the colors in the same manner. Teach the name of the color after its recognition.

3. Arrange a promiscuous assortment of colored papers on the table. Ask the pupils in turn to select the colors you point to on the color chart. If the pupil selects the right one let him pick it up. Do this until all the colors are chosen.

4. Designs 2–20 are made with round parquetry papers, but similar designs may be made of any size or shape — square, rectangular, triangular, oval, or elliptical. These round disks are marked with a letter, the initial letter of the color tint or shade. Thus R stands for red; O, Y, G, B, and V, for orange, yellow, green, blue, and violet. T stands for tint, and T' and T" for the first and second tints. S stands for shade, and S' and S" for the first and second shade of the color used. These designs are used by simply drawing one of the designs on the blackboard and having the pupils imitate it with the colored papers. Do this systematically with all the colors and combinations of colors.

5. Paste samples of the primary colors and intermediate colors, together with their tints and shades, on pieces of cardboard. Place these colored cards promiscuously along the blackboard rail. Point to a color on the color chart, and ask a pupil to find it among the cards. Point to two colors on the chart and ask the pupil to find both. In like manner point to three, four, and even five colors.

6. Place the color cards along the blackboard rail and ask the pupils to find the colors as you call them by name.

7. Hold a color card before the class for a moment, then remove the card. Ask a pupil to find it on the color chart. Ask the pupil to name the color.

8. The colored material collected by the pupils is studied by comparison with the color chart. The pupils look at the color of the material, judge what it is, and then verify by comparison with the color chart. Very little colored material can be found like the

pure spectrum scales. The great bulk is found among the tints, shades, broken colors and grays.

DRILL EXERCISES.

1. Place colored papers of the six primary colors and gray, including white and black, on the table. Point to the red on the color chart and have a pupil find it among the papers on the table. Do the same with yellow, blue, orange, green, violet, gray. Teach the name of each.

2. Hold a primary color before the class. Mary, find this color on the color chart. Find it in another place. What is the name of the color?

3. George, find red on the chart. Orange. Blue. Yellow. Green. Violet. Gray.

4. Place on the table a promiscuous assortment of the primary colors, gray, white and black. Paul, find blue. Mary, red. Edna, gray, etc., until all the colors are chosen.

5. Draw design 2 on the blackboard and let the pupils reproduce it in colored papers. Design 3. Design 4. Design 5. Design 6.

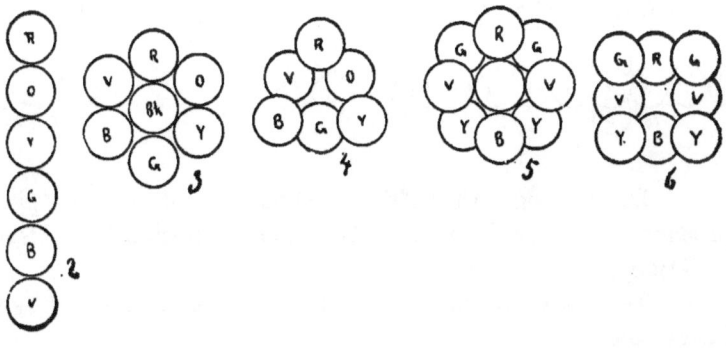

6. Teach the recognition of the tints and shades of each primary color. Not a particular tint or shade, but the general tint or shade.

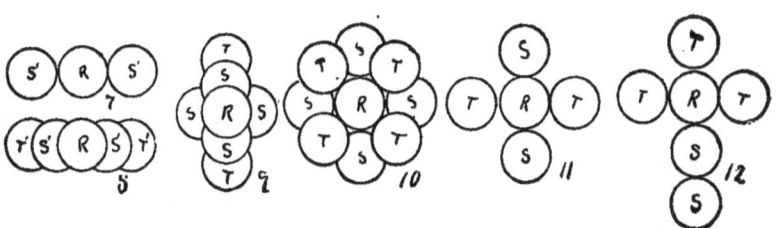

7. Draw design 7 on the blackboard and let the pupils reproduce it in colored papers. Design 8. Design 9. Design 10. Design 11. Design 12.

NOTE.— Each of the above designs is made of the first tint and shade of red. The teacher is to substitute any color in the place of red that she wishes to teach. The same also in designs 13-18.

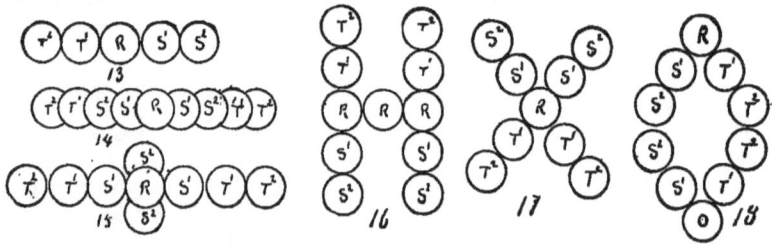

8. Draw design 13 on the blackboard and let the pupils reproduce it in colored papers. Design 14. Design 15. Design 16. Design 17. Design 18.

9. Teach the intermediate colors in the same manner as the primary colors.

AUGSBURG'S DRAWING. 159

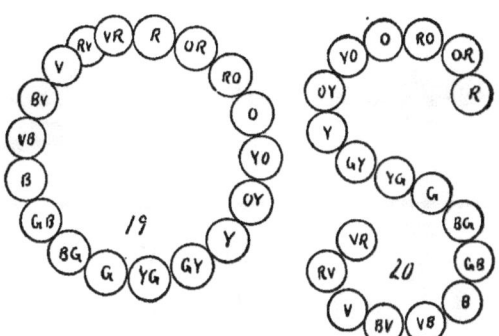

10. Place design 19 on the blackboard and let the pupils reproduce it in colored papers. Design 20.

NOTE.— Figs. 19 and 20 form complete color scales composed of the primary colors with two intermediate colors between.

CHAPTER XIV.

BRUSH DRAWING.

A child naturally sees an object as a whole — as a unit; but the moment he tries to reproduce it in drawing, the object as a unit disappears, and his attention is concentrated on the details. For example, the child may see a bird as a unit, but in an attempt to draw it he will separate the bird into many units; into the bill, head, tail, body, feathers, legs, feet, etc. These he will see separately and only imperfectly recognize their relation. To neutralize this tendency in children, and to lead them to represent the mass rather than the detail, to see the whole rather than the part, to recognize and tell the larger truth rather than the lesser, is the chief value of brush drawing. It is also an excellent preparation for water color painting.

Materials.— Common ink, a brush, and paper.

MEDIUMS.— Common ink is good, but drawing ink is better, being jet black. A gray may be made by mixing water with the ink. The violet, blue, warm gray, and cold gray of the color-box also make excellent mediums.

BRUSHES.— Number 3, 4, 5, or 6 round camel's hair brushes are the best. Number 3 is small and 4, 5, and 6 each a trifle larger than the number below it. Many prefer the Japanese brushes. One brush is sufficient.

PAPER.— Common drawing paper may be used. White is preferable.

Method of Teaching.— Simply show the pupils *how*, by making a drawing yourself, and then let them follow your example.

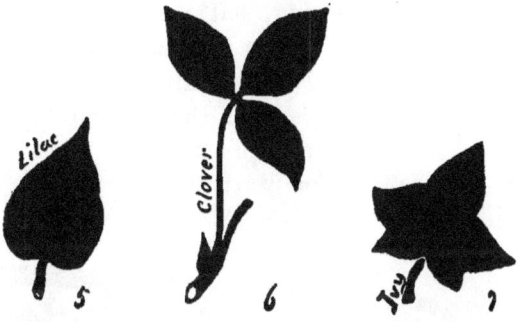

For instance, give each pupil a lilac leaf, Fig. 5. Pin or tack a sheet of paper to the blackboard or some other conspicuous place where the pupils can easily see it. Pin a lilac leaf to one corner of the paper, and with brush and ink draw or paint it, similar to Fig. 5. Let the pupils do the same with their leaf on their tablets.

Do not outline the leaf with a pencil, but rather work from within, outward. To outline the leaf and then fill in with ink, largely defeats the end in view. It is best to work without an outline when the objects are not of rigid proportion, and are of simple form. It is best in general, not to use the outline in such objects as leaves, buds, flowers, fruit, vegetables, trees, plants, birds, animals, and most natural objects, though this is not intended as an arbitrary rule. Often a few guiding lines, indicating directions and position, are necessary and helpful; but in general depend on the unaided brush.

Place a plant of simple outline, such as a rubber plant, Chinese lily, or calla lily, Fig. 8, in front of a light background, where the class can see it plainly, and then let the pupils draw it with brush and ink. Do not be content with one drawing, but make two, three, and even four. This can be done in ten minutes.

Many like to use a pen for very fine lines and details, and there is no objection to this, though, with practice, the brush is capable of quite as fine work as the pen.

Such objects as pears, lemons, a bunch of grapes, or a cluster of cherries are excellent as models for brush drawing, because of the strong characteristic outline; but such objects as an orange, apple or peach are not so good, because the character is not to such an extent in the outline. Only objects with strong characteristic outline should be chosen for first efforts.

List of Objects.—The following is a good list to choose from, though somewhat limited in extent.

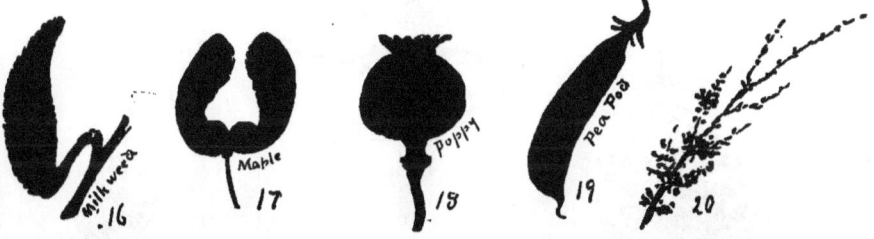

Grasses, seeds, and seed-pods, both green and dried, are among the very best sources for brush drawing. There are no better objects for this work than milkweed pods, box elder, and maple seeds, poppy capsules, dried grasses, and the like.

Nuts are both excellent and interesting subjects. The acorn,

peanut, clusters ot butternuts, walnuts, hickory nuts, hazel nuts, beech nuts, and horse-chestnuts are all good.

Heads of wheat, rye, oats, barley, and rice are graceful and interesting.

Vegetables and fruit are always at hand and many of them make good models. The following are the best: squashes, gourds, onions, turnips, carrots, radishes, and cucumbers; and among fruits, cherries, plums, pears, grapes, lemons, bananas, currants, and gooseberries are good.

Leaves are among the easiest and best models; nearly all kinds are good, especially those of simple form and smooth edges, like the lilac and ivy.

Trees are the most interesting of all. Almost any kind of tree is good for this purpose, providing it stands alone, with the sky for a background; it should stand out prominently. The maple, poplar, spruce, pine, oak, elm, plum, palm, bushes of all sorts, shrubs, and plants are all available. A mullein stalk is a fine model.

Bits of landscape are often very effective, such as a stump, dead trees, large stone, bunch of grass or rushes. A mountain, bluff or hill; an island or point of land; a gate, bars, tower, bridge, or ruins; an old barn, shed, shanty, cabin, or house; also all sorts of shipping, wharves, and piers.

Articles of china and earthern-ware have fine outlines and beautiful proportions; vases, pitchers, jugs, jars and lamps are the best.

Articles of wear, such as hats, caps, boots, shoes, slippers, and umbrellas, are very good.

The various tools found in the shops, garden, and kitchen are interesting to children, such as the hammer, hatchet, ax, knife, pincers, saw, hoe, rake, shovel, dipper, rolling-pin, kettle, etc.

166   AUGSBURG'S DRAWING.

Little things found in the pockets of boys, such as keys knives, fish-hooks, sinkers, nails, button-hooks, etc., are excellent

Stuffed animals, birds, and fishes are very interesting. There is no better way to gain the general form and proportion of an animal, bird, or insect, than through brush drawing. The aquarium is a good source for this work.

Take the class out Friday afternoon when the weather is fine and let them paint trees, bushes, rocks, and houses, as they appear in silhouette against the sky, especially when the objects are

between you and the light. This will be found a most interesting and effective use for brush drawing.

Brush drawing can be studied from pictures. Simple pictures

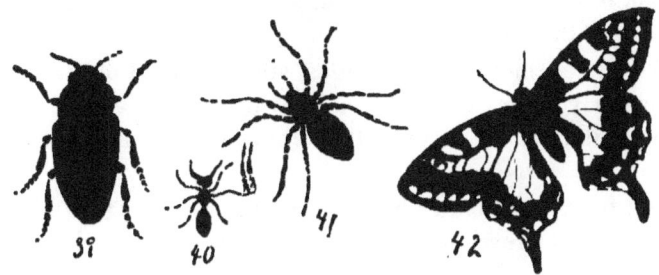

cut from magazines and papers and pasted on cardboard may be used for this purpose. Animals in action are especially interesting, also birds flying, and boys and girls playing.

Fog, haze, smoke, and storm, all tend to eliminate details, and make plain the general mass. On such days direct the attention of the pupils to distant objects and teach them to observe the shape of the mass.

Butterflies, moths, flies, beetles, etc., mounted on white cards, are peculiarly adapted for brush drawing. They can be mounted by the pupils themselves, and then they will be more interesting to them.

Cut from cardboard three inches square, a figure similar to Fig. 43. This figure may be laid on paper and marked around, and Figs. 44, 45, and 46 made from it. These designs differ only in the parts that are left black and white. Pupils may make designs similar to these, mark around them, and make four designs from each.

The principal historical units may be taught in this way.

DRILL EXERCISES.

1. Show pupils how to draw with brush and ink a lilac leaf. Let them draw a lilac leaf. An ivy leaf. Laurel leaf. Oak. Maple. Clover. Locust. Rose. Ash. Sorrel. Pear. Sweet pea. Beech. Virginia creeper. Sweet fern. Hemlock. Pine. Spruce.

2. Place a simple plant before the pupils and let them draw it.

3. At the proper time have a lesson on the pussy willows. Lilac buds. Alder catkins. Birch catkins. Buds of the poplar tree.

4. Choose some simple flower that you can find plentifully and use it in the drawing lesson.

AUGSBURG'S DRAWING.

5. Procure some milkweed pods for a drawing lesson. Some maple seeds. Some poppy capsules. Some peas in the pod.

6. Ask a pupil to procure a quart of acorns for use in the drawing class. A bag of peanuts. Some clusters of walnuts. A cluster of butternuts. A cluster of hazel nuts.

7. Procure some heads of wheat, rye, and barley, and let the pupils make a drawing of each and learn the difference between them. Use some oat heads for a drawing lesson. Some rice heads.

8. As opportunity presents use a squash for a model. A carrot. A radish. A pear. A bunch of grapes. A banana.

9. Take the class out Friday afternoon and make a brush drawing of a tree. A bush. A clump of trees. A dead tree. A large stone. An old ruin. An island. A point of rocks. A stump. A mullein stalk. A gate. A bridge.

10. Use for a drawing model a pitcher. A vase. A teapot. A jug. A cup.

11. Use a hat for a model. A cap. An umbrella. A ladies' hat.

12. Ask one of the boys to bring a hatchet to school for a model in drawing. A saw. A mallet. A hammer. A rake. A rolling pin. A knife.

13. A cart makes an excellent model. So does a wheel-barrow; a sled; a skate.

14. Let each boy and girl draw some article they have about them, such as a pin. Hair pin. Ribbon. Pocket-knife. Fish-hook. Sinker. Button-hook.

15. Ask a pupil who can to bring a mounted bird, fish, or reptile to school for a model.

16. The aquarium, with its fish, turtles, frogs, salamanders and shell fish, should be the source of many lessons.

17. Draw some object from the school window, such as a tree. Spire. Dome. House. Barn. Haystack. Cupola.

18. Many of the butterflies, moths, and beetles mounted by the class in nature study may be used in the drawing class.

19. Friday afternoon go to the river or lake and make a brush drawing of a boat. A pier. A point of rocks. Some bulrushes. A bridge. A mill.

20. Sketch a landscape on the blackboard and let the class make a brush drawing of it.

21. Cut from cardboard three inches square a design similar to Fig. 43 and let pupils make four brush drawings from it similar to designs 43–46:

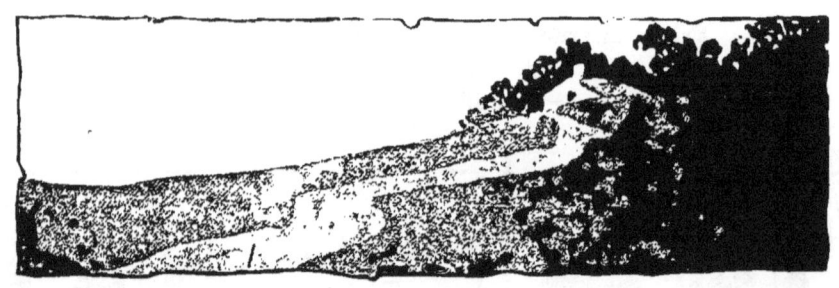

CHAPTER XV.

WATER COLORS.

Materials.—The materials necessary for work are a box of water colors, a pad of water color paper, a No. 6 camel's hair brush, a piece of linen or cotton cloth (old not new) and a small cup to hold water.

WATER COLORS.—A standard box of water colors should contain the six primary colors — red, orange, yellow, green, blue and violet, together with warm gray and cold gray. The colors should approximate those on the color chart and the colored papers.

WATER COLOR PAPER.— Pads $4\frac{1}{2}$ x 6 inches are large enough for first efforts, and after that a pad 6 x 9 may be used. 9 x 12 is the next larger pad.

WATER COLOR BRUSHES. — A No. 6 round camel's hair brush is perhaps the best for general work. They may be procured, however, larger or smaller if desired.

BLOTTER. — The linen or cotton cloth is to be used as a blotter to take the color from the brush, and to clean the box. Old and well-worn cloth is much better than new. The cloth should be folded neatly into a small pad.

WATER CUPS. — Each pupil should have a small cup to hold water. Small tin cups that set into each other and take up very little space, may be gotten, if uniformity is desired, otherwise, any cup will do.

General Facts about Water Colors. — The water color box should contain the six primary or standard colors — red, orange, yellow, green, blue, and violet, together with warm and cold gray. With the above colors nearly all shades, tints, and colors may be formed.

RED is a warm color. Red mixed with other colors tends to make them warmer. Red mixed with yellow makes an orange. Red mixed with blue makes a violet. The shade of red (red made darker) may be approximated by the admixture of warm gray.

ORANGE is the warmest color, and is the connecting link between red and yellow. Orange mixed with other colors tends to make them warmer and brighter. Warm gray added to orange will approximate the shade of orange.

YELLOW more than any other color represents light. It is the most luminous of colors. Yellow mixed with other colors tends to make them lighter and brighter. Yellow mixed with blue makes green. Warm gray mixed with yellow approximates the shade of yellow.

GREEN is a cold color as it tends toward blue, but light and bright as it tends toward yellow. Broken greens are obtained by the admixture of green with other colors, especially the grays.

BLUE is a receding color and represents coldness. Blue mixed with other colors tends to make them colder.

VIOLET is a very vivid color. Its shade may be approximated by the admixture of cold gray.

WARM GRAY and COLD GRAY are the mediums, through admixture with the above standard colors, by which we obtain the long range of broken colors commonly included under the head of browns, grays, broken greens, etc.

BLACK is made by adding red to cold gray.

Washes.—A wash is water tinted with color and then spread more or less evenly over the surface that is to be tinted or painted.

Preparing the Wash.—The manner of preparing the wash is as follows: (1) Dip the brush in water and press it into one of the compartments of the water color box. Do this until you have enough color for the wash. (2) Rub up a little color with the brush and mix it with the water in the cover. The wash is ready now to apply to the paper. Often the wash is taken directly from the color cake.

Applying the Wash.—Grasp the water color tablet with the left hand and incline it at an angle of about 30 or 40 degrees, as in Fig. 5. Dip the brush in the wash and apply with a *full or saturated brush working from the top downward. Keep the brush full of the color wash.*

The superfluous color that is left at the bottom of the design may be removed by the brush. To do this, first place the point of the brush on the cloth, to draw the color from it, and then the superfluous color on the paper may be taken up by merely touching it with the dried brush.

The wash dries in a few minutes, when another wash may be placed, at pleasure, over the whole, or a part of the picture or design. The wash may be repeated any number of times. These superimposed washes constitute the water color picture or design.

Learning the Colors.—The best way of learning color is by working in color — by using color — by comparing one color with another. Simply learning the names is not enough. We must learn the colors so that we know them as we know the face of a friend.

Plan of Work.—The general plan here given for learning color, is as follows:

1. An orderly and systematic course in washes. There is no better way of learning color than to spread it over a comparatively large surface, in varying washes, forming pleasing designs.
2. Painting objects of simple form and color.

THE FIRST LESSON.

Children love to work in bright colors and with the full strength of the color. It is well, then, to begin with an object that is bright in color and simple in its parts, such as the flags, Figs 7–14.

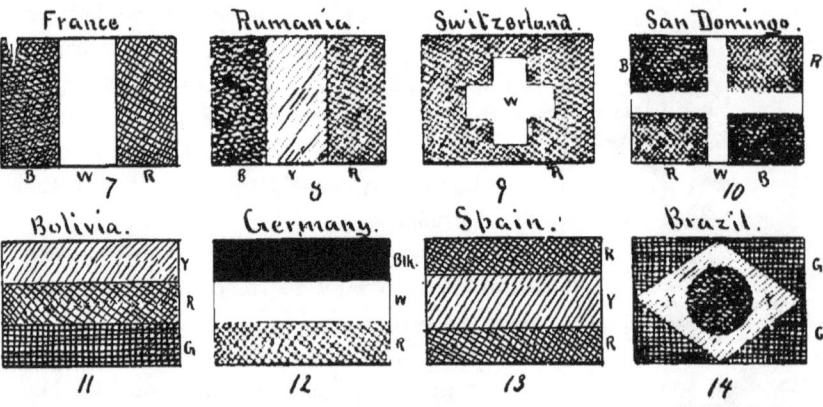

These flags have been chosen because of their simplicity both of form and color. An excellent plan of conducting the first lessons in water colors is as follows:

Preparation.—(1) Choose as many pupils to help you as you have rows of seats in your school-room. We will say six.

Each of these "captains" will look after one row of seats, supplying and collecting material, and during the first lessons, assisting the other pupils in their work.

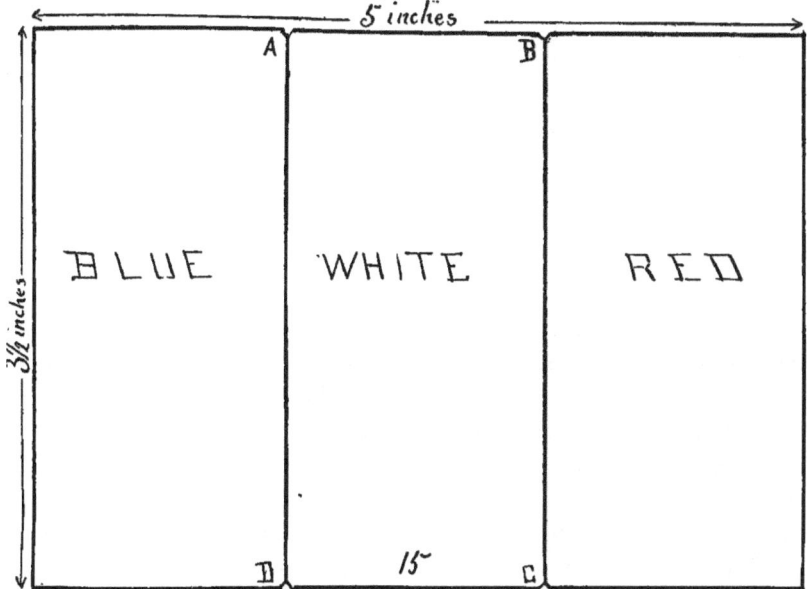

(2) Cut six pieces of cardboard 3½ x 5 inches, which is the size of the flags, Figs. 7-14.

To paint Fig. 7, the French flag, divide the cardboards into three equal parts, to correspond to the stripes in the French flag. (3) Give each captain a cardboard and let him mark out a flag for each pupil in his row. This is done by laying the card on each pad and marking around it with a pencil, and then marking the stripes. If notches are cut in the card, as *A*, *B*, *C*, and *D*, Fig. 15, the position of the stripes will be marked automatically. (4) Show the captains how to paint the flag and then during the regular lesson let them help the pupils in their row.

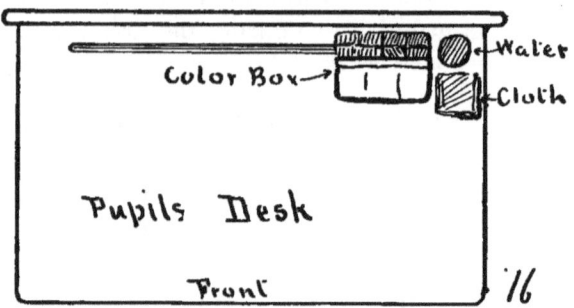

Have each pupil arrange his color box, water cup, and pad of cloth, on his desk, as indicated in Fig. 16.

Before beginning the regular lesson, pin a piece of paper in a conspicuous place and let the pupils see you paint the flag, then without further instruction let them do the same. Do not talk or instruct too much. Let the pupils paint without more interruption than is necessary. Do not expect accuracy in these lessons, nor neat, clean work. The first exercises will necessarily be dauby. After the first wash is dry, a second, or even a third wash may be put on, if the color is not strong enough.

The white cross in the flag of Switzerland, and the blue circle in the flag of Brazil, may be cut out, and then these flags may be easily marked on the pads.

Black for the flag of Germany may be made by adding a little red to cold gray.

The aim in these flag lessons is to give the pupils opportunity to become used to colors and to learn how to handle them, and at the same time it gives a lesson in strong washes.

Fig. 17 is composed of two squares, a 4 inch square, and a 3 inch square. The 4 inch square is common to all the figures. The 3 inch square is cut into a design which is laid inside of the large square.

The use of these square cards is to multiply designs easily and quickly, for the pupils to paint in water colors. The design is made by laying the large square on the water color pad and

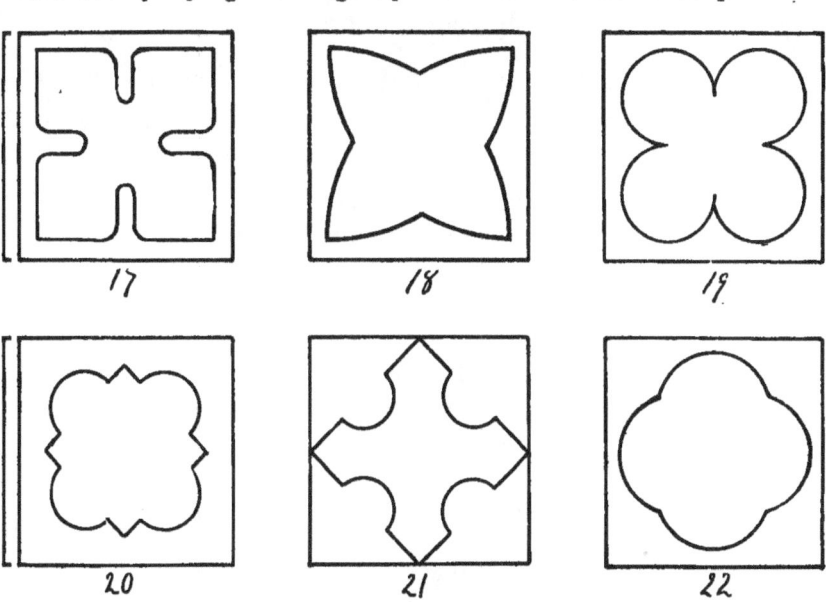

marking around it, and then laying the smaller design inside of this large square and marking around it, thus making the design. The teacher, the "captains" or the pupils can do this work. If preferred, the pupils may make their own designs, only this takes much time and it is color we are studying in this lesson.

The designs are painted by passing *one wash over the entire design, and after this is dry, a second wash over one of the parts,* as shown by Fig. 23.

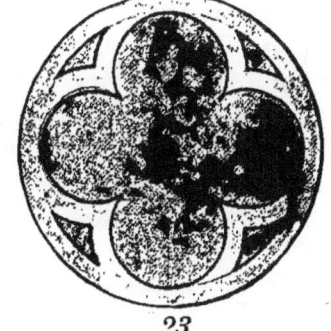

180   AUGSBURG'S DRAWING.

25

The aim of this work is also to teach color. By going over these or similar designs in a systematic way, an excellent drill in color is given, and this, in connection with the painting of objects, forms a complete outline of study in this subject.

A pupil, after he knows what to do, can paint four of these designs in one lesson, one on each side of two pieces of paper.

Painting Objects.—The thought, *we cannot represent all*, should be prominently in mind when painting objects. We can tell the truth, but not the whole truth. We can represent thoughts about the object, but we cannot represent all the thoughts. We cannot represent everything we see, but we can a part. We may choose certain leading truths and represent them as near as we can, and in proportion as we represent them truthfully we will have a good drawing.

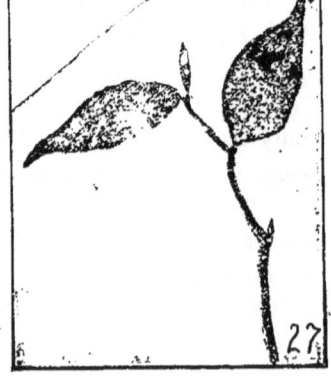

The artist seeks to represent the
    form,
    local color,
    shadow,

> general shade,
> detailed shade,
> high lights,
> reflex lights,
> shade values,
> color values,

and to represent them all truthfully; but with little children we cannot expect so much.

With little children we may get fairly good results if we aim at *form* and *local color*, as in Figs. 25 and 26.

Or the *form*, *local color*, and *high lights*, as in Fig. 28.

Or the *form*, *local color*, and *shadow*, as in Fig. 24.

Any of the above, truthfully rendered, will have the elements of a good picture.

For first efforts, the form must be simple and the color distinct, as in the banana and lemon. Bright colors that can be easily recognized should characterize the objects that the child paints. Gray colors are puzzling to children. Observe there is no shade on the banana — only form and color. It is the same with the trees, the cherries, the leaves, the pussy willow, carnation, dandelion and walnuts—form and local color, no more.

The Wet Wash is placing a wash over a surface that is already moist or wet. When this is done the color spreads and blends together without leaving hard lines and edges.

Fig. 29 was painted by moistening the surface of the drawing with water, and then dropping the color on it from the end of the brush and letting it all blend together.

The carrot, Fig. 30, was painted in the same manner. The eye spots were added after the wash was dry.

Many objects with two colors blended together, like the apple, Fig. 31, may be represented as follows:

Paint the object with the lighter wash, and after it is dry, moisten the surface with water and then "drop" in the stronger color from the end of the brush, while the surface is still wet. The color will spread and blend itself.

Autumn leaves may be painted in this manner, quite easily. The veins may be added after the wash is dry, or may be taken out with the dried brush, while the wash is wet.

Trees may be painted in one mass without shade or shadow, aiming at the form and local color only, as shown by Figs. 34–37. Even small children attain considerable success in this work.

Objects Suitable to Paint.— Among the fruits are bananas, lemons, bright colored apples, pears, tomatoes, plums, peaches, currants, cherries and grapes.

Among the vegetables are the radish, carrot, cucumber, pumpkin, crook neck squash and gourds.

Nearly all flowers, simple in form and color, are excellent. Some of the best are: sunflower, yellow Marguerite, yellow daisy, many pansies, sweet pea, some poppies, water lily bud, rose bud,

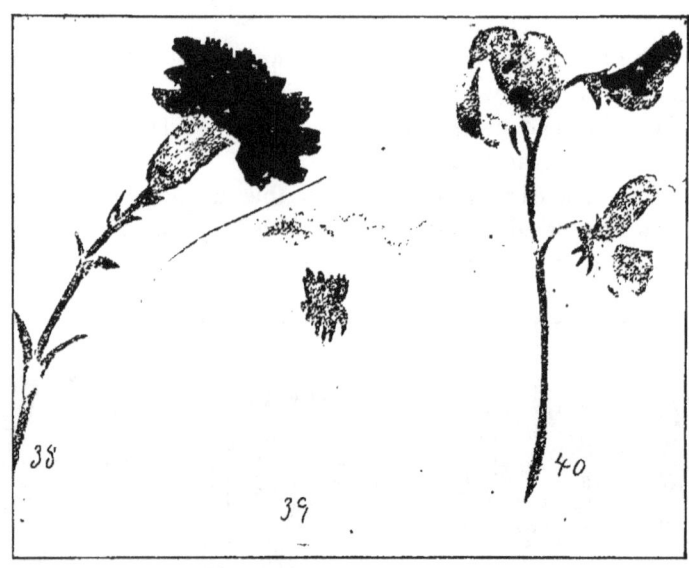

wild rose, tulip, buttercup, iris, marigold, anemone, bluet, daffodil, forget-me-not, etc.

Grasses are good to paint and many of them are simple and easy: the clover, sorrel, flax, oats, alfalfa, rushes; especially the sprouting bean, pea, corn and grain.

Trees are among the best subjects for painting, providing only the form and local color are reproduced; otherwise they are too difficult. The following trees are good: maple, lilac, hickory, chestnut, walnut, butternut, poplar, oak, elm, willow, ash, fruit trees, beech, birch, basswood, pine, spruce, eucalyptus and palm.

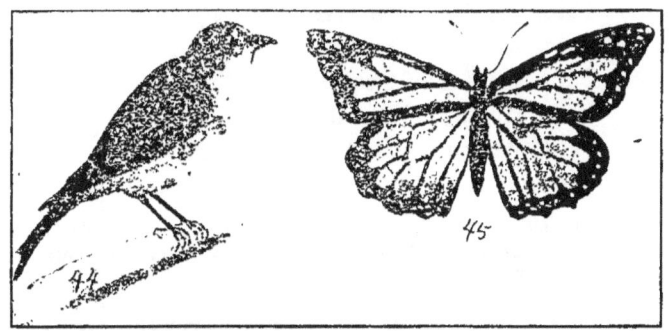

Some birds, like the bluebird, robin, oriole, yellow birds and black birds, may be used, if good stuffed specimens can be found.

Butterflies are excellent. Their bright colors and strong markings make them especially adapted for this work. Butterflies can be procured already mounted, but the children can mount them very easily by placing a drop of mucilage on a white card and placing the body on it. Do not flatten the wings to the card, but allow them to project at an angle from the card surface.

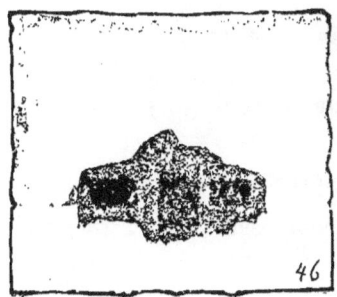  

DRILL EXERCISES.

1. Paint a picture of the flag of France, Figs. 7 and 15.
2. Paint a picture of the flag of Roumania, Fig. 8.
3. Paint a picture of the flag of Switzerland, Fig. 9.
4. Paint a picture of the flag of San Domingo, Fig. 10.
5. Paint the flag of Bolivia.
6. Paint the flag of Germany.
7. Paint the flag of Spain.
8. Paint the flag of Brazil.
9. Paint design 17 in two light washes of red. Paint in two heavy washes of red.

NOTE.— The shade of red, orange, yellow, and green is approximated by the admixture of warm gray. The shade of blue and violet is approximated by the admixture of cold gray.

10. Paint design 18 in two tints of orange. In two shades of orange.
11. Paint design 19 in two tints of yellow. In two shades of yellow.
12. Paint design 20 in two tints of green. In two strong washes of green. In two shades of green.
13. Paint design 21 in two tints of blue. Two heavy washes of blue.
14. Paint design 22 in two tints of violet. Two heavy washes of violet.
15. Paint design 17 in two tints of warm gray. In two heavy washes of warm gray.
16. Paint design 18 in two tints of cold gray. In two heavy washes of cold gray.

NOTE.— Design 23 may be cut from one piece of cardboard 3½ inches square.

17. Paint design 23 in a wash composed of cold gray and orange mixed together.

 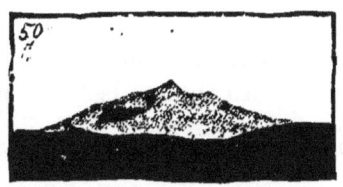 

Note.—In the following problems let the pupils paint the object, aiming at the form and local color only. They are to paint the objects direct without an outline drawing.

18. Let the pupils paint a spray of leaves similar to Fig. 27.
19. Let the pupils paint a banana. A lemon. A yellow apple. A green apple. A yellow pear. A tomato. Two plums. A cluster of cherries.
20. Let each pupil paint a radish. A carrot. A cucumber. A pumpkin.
21. Let each pupil paint a sunflower. A yellow Marguerite. A rosebud. A buttercup. An iris. A forget-me-not. A spray of sweet peas. A dandelion.
22. Let the pupils paint a clover leaf. A spray of leaves. A grass stalk. A sprouting bean with its root.
23. Have the pupils paint a cluster of walnuts, butternuts, hickory nuts, or hazel nuts.
24. Paint a maple tree. A live oak tree. A white oak tree. A palm tree. A plum tree. A eucalyptus tree. An acacia tree. A pine, spruce, or hemlock tree. A beech, butternut, hickory, or walnut tree. A lilac, willow, elm, ash, or basswood tree.
25. Paint a mounted blue bird. Yellow bird. A black bird. A butterfly.
26. Paint a Chinese lantern. A Jack-o'-lantern.

Note.— Paint the following objects in two colors, using a wet wash and letting the colors flow together.

188   AUGSBURG'S DRAWING.

27. Paint a red and yellow apple. A red and yellow pear. A red and yellow peach. An autumn leaf. A pansy.

NOTE.— Paint the following objects in form, local color, and shadow, similar to Figs. 4 and 24.

28. Pussy willow. Catkins. Dandelion. Carnation. California poppy. Spray of pepper leaves. Spray of maiden hair fern.

NOTE.— Find a suitable landscape similar to Figs. I, 2, 47, 48, 49, 50, and 51, and Friday afternoon take the children out and let them make a picture of it. If they can see some one else do this to show them what to look for, excellent results may be gained. The following are suitable objects for this work: A gate, bars, rock, an island, a point projecting into water, a stump, old bridge, cabin. shanty, old ruins, stone wall, etc.

www.ingramcontent.com/pod-product-compliance
Lightning Source LLC
Chambersburg PA
CBHW020847160426
43192CB00007B/825